DEEMED UNSUITABLE

*Blacks from Oklahoma Move to the Canadian Prairies
in Search of Equality in the Early 20th Century
Only to Find Racism in their New Home*

R. Bruce Shepard

UMBRELLA

PRESS

Toronto

DEDICATION

*To the memory of my mother, E. Mary Shepard,
who understood the true nature of prejudice.*

DEEMED UNSUITABLE

*Blacks From Oklahoma Move to the Canadian Prairies in Search of Equality in
the Early 20th Century Only to Find Racism in their New Home*

Publisher: *Ken Pearson*
Editor: *Olive Koyama*
Design :   *Sona Communication, Sarah Rashid*

Cover Photo: Settlers in the Creek Nation, Oklahoma
(Archives and Manuscripts, Division of the Oklahoma Historical Society)

*The Publisher acknowledges the assistance of the Multicultural Program of the
Department of Canadian Heritage.*

Canadian Cataloguing in Publication Data

Shepard, R. Bruce
     Deemed unsuitable

Includes bibliographical references and index.
ISBN 1-895642-19-1

1. Blacks - Alberta - History - 20th century.   2. Blacks - Saskatchewan - History -
20th century.   3. African-Americans - Oklahoma - History - 20th century.
4. Racism - Alberta.   5. Racism - Saskatchewan.   6. Alberta - Ethnic relations.
7. Saskatchewan - Ethnic relations.   8. Alberta - Emigration and immigration.
9. Saskatchewan - Emigration and immigration.   10. Oklahoma - Emigration and
immigration.   I. Title.
JV7285.A3S5   1997   325.2'089607307123   C95-932919-6

A *kennyp* Publication

Manufactured in Canada

UMBRELLA PRESS
56 Rivercourt Blvd.
Toronto, ON. M4J 3A4

Telephone: (416) 696-6665
Fax: (416) 696-9189

TABLE OF CONTENTS

PREFACE   iv

INTRODUCTION   1

Chapter One: COLOUR, RACE AND SLAVERY   5

Chapter Two: RACISM MIGRATES WESTWARD   19

Chapter Three: STATEHOOD AND SEGREGATION   34

Chapter Four: THE POLITICS OF RACISM   50

Chapter Five: RACISM ON THE NORTHERN PLAINS   66

Chapter Six: CANADA'S DIPLOMATIC RACISM   86

Chapter Seven: THE ONGOING STRUGGLE   102

CONCLUSION   CHANGING THE WORLD   121

BIBLIOGRAPHY   127

INDEX   147

PREFACE

The difficulty lies not in the new ideas, but in escaping from the old ones, which ramify into every corner of our mind.

— John Maynard Keynes

The Underground Railroad is a well-known chapter in the racial history of North America. This secret anti-slavery network helped thousands of African Americans flee their bondage for freedom in Canada. Yet few people in either country are aware that there was another African-American migration northward.

Between 1905 and 1912 over one thousand black men, women, and children migrated from the United States to the plains region of Canada. They came mainly from Oklahoma, although some were from Kansas and Texas. They settled in the Canadian provinces of Saskatchewan and Alberta.

This is one story of those migrations.

Because of its racial basis, our story is also much more. Too many Canadian studies of the people who have chosen to settle here begin only with their arrival in Canada. This study seeks the origins of the African-American migration, and finds them in the racist attitudes of white America. The white Canadian response to the black migrants is also scrutinized, and similarities in the racial attitudes of the two North American countries are shown in stark relief. They reveal the longevity and adaptability of a white European racism, elements of which can be traced back centuries, and of the virulence of a white British strain.

The racial basis of this story gives it a contemporary significance as well. In the United States, the status of African Americans and the relations between blacks and whites are part of a continuing debate on civil rights. All too often this discussion takes place in an historical vacuum. Our study may help to fill this gap, even in a small way. If nothing else, the story of the black migration to western Canada should present both white and black Americans with the sobering picture of American citizens abandoning their country because it failed them.

Canadians too are currently engaged in a debate about the racial composition of their country. Non-white immigration to Canada has grown considerably in recent decades, and has triggered considerable hostility toward visible-minority immigrants.

In both the United States and Canada, there seems to be little historical perspective to the discussion. Ideally this study will show Canadians that non-white immigration is not a new question in their country. It should also show them that, however much they pride themselves on their ethnic and racial tolerance, they still have not confronted the latent racism in their society.

Race is a dated, quasi-scientific term used to describe the general divisions of humanity according to physical characteristics. Racism is the belief or attitude that certain people are an inferior type of humanity because of their biological inheritance. Both words are emotion-charged and must be employed with care.

Writers dealing with the origins, development, and expression of such ideas can rightly expect to have their own value system questioned. This is especially the case when the writer is perceived to be white, and the subjects of the writing are black. Simply put, can a supposedly white man tell this story?

The author recognizes that the question demands an answer. That answer is yes; an apparently white man can tell this story.

There are three reasons for this answer. The first is that while the story focuses upon the black migration, it is really about white racism. The motivations and decisions of the African-American migrants to Canada cannot be understood apart from the white racist societies in which they lived. The author is considered to be white, and is propelled by the need to confront that same racism which is all too much a part of his heritage. After all, the great African-American leader Malcolm X once advised whites that if they wanted to help fight racism they should study their own past.

The second reason for this answer is that the full story of the black trek from Oklahoma to Canada needs to be told. A few commentators have touched upon the migration, but no one has provided a full account. The author is obliged to present his findings to the public, lest the story remain buried, its perspective unavailable to the modern reader.

Third, nothing prevents a scholar of a different ethnic or social background from researching the topic again, and presenting a revised view. History is not a thing waiting to be found, but a process of enquiry to be repeatedly applied as new data and fresh perspectives become available. The major problem is not overcoming one's own ethnicity, but trying to understand the thinking of people in different historical eras than one's own.

Racism is a product of violent emotions. Those feelings are often expressed in coarse language and horrifying deeds. It is unfortunate, but necessary, to repeat some of that language, and to describe some of those actions, so that the reader will understand the historical drama as it unfolds. Some people will be shocked by those words and descriptions. They should be. They should also realize that their reaction is a small but important measure of how far we have come in the area of race relations in ensuing decades.

Neither Canadians nor Americans are as familiar with each other as they should be. Consequently, the author has seen fit to include descriptions and explanations of geography, historical evolution, and politics that some readers may find unnecessary. The writer begs their indulgence in the cause of mutual understanding.

This book is intended for Canadians and Americans, blacks and whites, who want to learn more about their mutual past. It is not weighed down with the usual ballast of footnotes, a burden which has done much to remove history from its rightful place as a branch of literature. Someone once said that reading footnotes was like running downstairs to answer the door in the middle of the night when you were on your honeymoon. The author has tried to keep such interruptions to a minimum.

The author was trained in the history departments of two of the leading western Canadian universities. The research was conducted according to the professional standards set by those institutions and a list of sources appears at the end of the book. Academics, their students, or anyone else wishing to more formally evaluate the evidence upon which this story is based are directed to the author's thesis for the University of Saskatchewan, Department of History, and to his articles in academic journals in both Canada and the United States. These publishers have kindly assented to the appearance of portions of the articles in this book:

"North to the Promised Land: Black Migration to the Canadian Plains," *Chronicles of Oklahoma,* Vol. 66, No. 3 (Fall, 1988). Oklahoma Historical Society, Oklahoma City, Oklahoma.

"The Origins of the Oklahoma Black Migration to the Canadian Plains," *Canadian Journal of History,* Vol. 23 (April, 1988). Department of History, University of Saskatchewan, Saskatoon, Saskatchewan.

"The Little 'White' Schoolhouse: Racism in a Saskatchewan Rural School," *Saskatchewan History,* Vol. 39, No. 3 (Autumn, 1986). Saskatchewan Archives Board, University of Saskatchewan, Saskatoon, Saskatchewan.

"Plain Racism: The Reaction Against Oklahoma Black Immigration to the Canadian Plains", *Prairie Forum,* Vol. 10, No. 2 (Fall, 1985). Canadian Plains Research Center, University of Regina, Regina, Saskatchewan.

"Diplomatic Racism: The Canadian Government and Black Migration from Oklahoma, 1905-1912," *Great Plains Quarterly,* Vol. 3, No. 1 (Winter, 1983). Center for Great Plains Studies, University of Nebraska, Lincoln, Nebraska.

The editors of these journals, and the anonymous reviewers who critiqued the articles prior to publication, are first on a list of individuals and organizations to be thanked for helping to bring the material presented here into the public forum. Much of the information which appeared in the articles was also presented to scholarly conferences, and the organizers of those events together with fellow panelists and those who attended helped to shape the final product.

These articles, and this manuscript, are based upon research for a graduate degree from the University of Saskatchewan, a school whose History Department inspires its students with the example of scholarly excellence. The author will always be grateful to his colleagues in Saskatoon for allowing him the opportunity to complete his work with them. In addition to these teachers, Marshall Whelan and Lydia Friesen deserve mention for their help with the translation which appears in chapter five.

The original supervisor of the research was Brian Jenkins, now of Bishop's University, who exercised his considerable editorial skills to divest the original dissertation of its many rough edges. The late Geoffrey Bilson completed the supervision with firm direction and quiet dignity. The Canadian scholarly community lost one of its finest practitioners with his untimely passing.

Graduate dissertations are not books, even though students' egos try to tell them otherwise. A great deal more research and several new drafts were required before the work was presentable to the public. Many people and institutions have helped in this long process, especially the archivists, librarians, and staff of the various repositories which were consulted on both sides of the international boundary. The author also gratefully acknowledges a multicultural research grant from the former Saskatchewan Department of Culture and Youth, a multicultural research grant from the Canadian Department of the Secretary of State, and a research travel award from the Canadian Plains Research Centre of the University of Regina.

Many people spent a great deal of time over numerous cups of coffee while the author developed his ideas. They have all been thanked individually, but a few special contributions deserve to be noted. Selwyn Murray of the University of Regina read the manuscript, offered many useful criticisms, and provided advice and guidance at crucial junctures. His continuing friendship is also a source of inspiration. Ahmad Azzahir of the Akephran Institute, Minneapolis, Minnesota, in a rare display of scholarly cooperation, shared his findings on the Eldon, Saskatchewan, community with me. During our undergraduate years together, Selwyn, Ahmad, and Eleuthan Noel, currently of New York City, helped to educate an ignorant, middle class, supposedly white Canadian on the international effects of racism.

This manuscript has been read in whole or in part by a number of individuals and scholars whose suggestions, comments and thoughts have been noted, if not always followed. My sincere thanks go to Paul Sharp, President Emeritus of the University of Oklahoma; Tom Isern of North Dakota State University; and Garin Burbank of the University of Winnipeg. I am also grateful to James St. G. Walker of the University of Waterloo; and Les Irwin of Arizona State University. I am also grateful to Jean Burnet of the Ontario Historical Society.

My father-in-law, Donald Lehman, of Regina, Saskatchewan, provided me with a detailed critique. Special thanks also goes to O.D. Larmer, of Regina who read the manuscript in its entirety. Even with the help of these friends and colleagues there may be errors and omissions, and for these the author assumes full responsibility.

Larry Hill of Toronto, Ontario, deserves to be noted for his encouragement, and for having put me in touch with a sympathetic publisher. That individual, Ken Pearson, Publisher of Umbrella Press, has displayed considerable understanding in guiding a novice author through the publication of his first book. Olive Koyama has proven to be a formidable, and demanding editor for which any author would be grateful.

I am most particulary grateful to Mrs. B. Edwards and Mrs. M. Mapp of Amber Valley and Mr. and Mrs. M. Hooks of Breton, Alberta, who in August 1983 shared with me their recollections of their pioneer days. I also appreciate the assistance of Mr. Murray Mayes of North Battleford, Saskatchewan, for keeping up to date on his energetic family.

My final debts are to my family. My children, Kirk and Heather, have tolerated their father's absences, even if they did not always understand the reasons for them. My hope is that this work will play a small part in creating a better society for them to live in. My wife Donna has typed, read, and criticized this work through its various manifestations as a thesis, as scholarly articles, and now as a manuscript. My amazement only grows at her ability to tolerate this "paper mistress" which has lived with us throughout most of our married life.

R. Bruce Shepard
Diefenbaker Canada Centre
University of Saskatchewan
Saskatoon, Saskatchewan

P. C. 1324

AT THE GOVERNMENT HOUSE AT OTTAWA.

PRESENT:

HIS EXCELLENCY

IN COUNCIL:

His Excellency in Council, in virtue of the provisions of Sub-Section (c) of Section 38 of the Immigration Act, is pleased to Order and it is hereby Ordered as follows:-

For a period of one year from and after the date hereof the landing in Canada shall be and the same is prohibited of any immigrants belonging to the Negro race, which race is deemed unsuitable to the climate and requirements of Canada.

To Interior 15 Aug. 1911

Wilfrid Laurier

approved Grey Aug 12/11

The "Deemed Unsuitable" Order-in-Council

INTRODUCTION

> For a period of one year from and after the date hereof the landing in Canada shall be and the same is prohibited of any immigrants belonging to the Negro race, which race is deemed unsuitable to the climate and requirements of Canada.
> — Canada, Government of Canada,
> Order-in-Council no. 1324,
> 12 August 1911.

North America has a colour problem. The problem is racism. The colour is white.

White racism is entrenched in North American society. It has a long ancestry, and has shown itself in different ways in the various regions of the continent. On the Great Plains, white racism has expressed itself as a form of exclusion.

During the settlement era, white homesteaders, on both sides of the forty-ninth parallel, went to considerable lengths to exclude blacks from the region. Black settlers attempting to make their homes in the Indian Territory discovered that white racism had preceded them to what would later become Oklahoma. Between one thousand and fifteen hundred blacks then turned north, only to find another variety of white racism thriving on the Canadian Plains.

The pioneer societies on North America's Great Plains responded similarly to black immigration because of their common European inheritance, particularly its British variant. There was a deep colour prejudice in British society even before the ancestors of Americans and Anglo-Canadians left for the New World. Black

1

had become an overwhelmingly negative symbol with profound sexual and religious connotations.

The major British confrontation with Africa, and what they took to be black-skinned people, occurred at the same time as Britain's colonies in the Caribbean and North America were demanding a continuous and cheap supply of labour. In spite of their own progress toward greater individual liberty the British reverted to the ancient practice of slavery to meet the colonial demand for labour. The British were able to legitimize the use of Africans as chattels because their racism encouraged them to believe that dark-skinned people were a lesser form of humanity. Black was a badge of inferiority to the British and their colonial descendants, and became the mark of slavery.*

Once established, slavery became the economic and social foundation of society in the southern United States. It flourished and became so entrenched that in 1861 white southerners went to war to defend it as part of their way of life. This white southern rebellion against the American republic was defeated, but it left a colour caste legacy that still stains the country.

Freed from the shackles of slavery after 1865, African Americans pursued happiness in a quest for land and liberty. Unable to fulfil their dreams in the older southern states, thousands of blacks joined their white fellow citizens heading west. One destination was the Indian Territory, where federal policies provided an opportunity to obtain land.

African Americans who would later move to the Canadian Plains were part of this westward movement. They were members of the proud, defiant, black phalanx which moved to the Indian Territory, and later Oklahoma, rather than accept racial segregation in the older southern states. They quickly discovered that the white southerners who had also moved to the region were determined to impose racist social and political policies in the new state.

The racial clash made Oklahoma's formative years bitter and bloody. White racists won the battle, and proceeded to implement segregation in public facilities, and to deprive African Americans

---

* An excellent analysis of the British contact with Africa and the origins of colonial North American racism is found in Winthrop D. Jordan, *White over Black: American Attitudes Toward the Negro, 1550-1812.* Baltimore: Penguin Books, 1969.

of the right to vote. African Americans fought these developments and protested their implementation, but to no avail. The failure of justice sparked a black migration to the Canadian Plains. Once again, African Americans showed that they would rather move than accept white racism.

Unfortunately for the black settlers white racism is a hardy weed, equally at home on the northern plains. White settlers on the Canadian Plains quickly showed that they suffered from the same racist myths as did white Americans. They sent up a chorus of protest against the black immigration. Business groups across the region led the campaign to keep the African Americans out of Canada. Newspapers covering the migration spread and reinforced racist stereotypes.

The Canadian federal government responded to Western Canada's cries for racial exclusion. Canadian immigration officials investigated the issue, and tried to deprive African Americans of information about the Canadian Plains. They also tried to deter the black settlers with rigorous medical examinations, even going so far as to try to bribe their own medical authorities to reject the African Americans. These methods were at best haphazard and eventually the Government of Canada sent two agents to Oklahoma to try to stop the migration. The second agent was himself an African American, and he was instrumental in ending the black trek.

For a brief period the Canadian government was uncertain that their African-American agent would succeed in stemming the tide. Just to be certain, the Canadian authorities approved an order-in-council barring people of African descent from entering the country.* When the agent's success became apparent the regulation was quietly withdrawn; the fact that it was approved at all shows how determined white Canadians were to exclude blacks from settling on the Canadian Plains.

The African Americans who made it past Canada's colour bar carved out new lives in the northern dominion. They worked their land, found jobs in the cities, and fought in their new country's wars. Their descendants still live and work in the region and are

---

*An order-in-council is a regulation approved by a federal or provincial cabinet, and has the force of law.

increasingly found across the country. The African Americans sank deep roots into Canada in order to survive the icy blasts of white Canadian racism.

Chapter One
COLOUR, RACE, AND SLAVERY

Margaret Mead:	Now, it is not good for people's character . . .
James Baldwin:	To be identified with angels.
Margaret Mead:	— to look like angels; it makes them behave very badly.
James Baldwin:	That's very strange, because the root of it is somewhere there, it seems to me, and that's deeper, I suppose, isn't it, than one would like to think?
Margaret Mead:	That's terribly, terribly deep, I think.
James Baldwin:	Deeper than churches.

— Margaret Mead and James Baldwin,
A Rap on Race, 1971.

Until the modern era of global migration the various European peoples generally had light complexions. For such people the colour white became a symbol of who they were. Like peoples the world over, Europeans saw themselves as essentially good. White was, therefore, a colour of goodness to them, as well as cleanliness and light. It also became the colour of their God, and his servants.

For Europeans the colour black was a way of visually and verbally expressing their opposite. It was the colour of everything

5

which they were not, the reverse of how they saw themselves. Black was the colour of evil and of sin. It could also represent sickness and death. Black was the colour of the Devil and his minions.*

Devil imagery was a factor in the development of white racism because it combined the ideas of blackness, sex, and sin. The combination was particularly powerful because each of the individual elements generated strong emotions. Its power was further increased because the image of the Devil was a visual one, and could be memorized and recalled when triggered by an event, word, or phrase: a crucial factor in an era when most people were illiterate. One early Church council recounted that the Devil's sinful nature found expression in his physical form. Among other things he was black, had a huge phallus and smelled bad. **

A particularly virulent form of white-European racism took root in the British Isles with important consequences for North America. Except for the Scandinavian peoples, the British had among the lightest complexions in the world. Their acute awareness of this fact is revealed in the principal language of Britain. English is a language at once forthright and capable of rich imagery, and black and white are two of the most powerful words in it. These two words are a means of expressing deeply felt emotions, and of conveying basic beliefs. In English, black and white are fundamental opposites.

The British did not indulge in the fanciful descriptions of wild sexual orgies with the Devil found in some parts of medieval Europe. He did, however, make an increasing number of appear-

---

* The image of the dark-skinned Devil has not died out completely. In 1987, an Italian-Canadian group donated a dark-skinned Lucifer statue to a Toronto church, but it was removed to the rectory in 1991 when some parishioners complained that it was insulting. A spokesperson for the group which had donated the statue was upset because "A devil is supposed to be dark ...." Calgary *Herald*, 2 November, 1991.

** The importance of perceptions of the Devil to the creation of modern racial stereotypes is revealed throughout Jeffrey Burton Russell's excellent three-volume history of the Devil. See *The Devil: Perceptions of Evil From Antiquity to Primitive Christianity* Ithaca: Cornell University Press, 1977; *Satan: The Early Christian Tradition* Ithaca, 1981; and *Lucifer: The Devil in the Middle Ages* Ithaca, 1984. It was the Council of Toledo in A.D. 447 which described the Devil in these revealing terms *Lucifer*, p.69, n.13.

ances in the British Isles as the Middle Ages gave way to the Early Modern era. The social and economic tensions associated with this change found expression in religious terms. As society transformed itself, witchcraft, including visits from the Devil, became an increasingly common charge in Tudor and Stuart Britain. At the same time a new secular outlook, which was a key element in the social and economic changes taking place, gave rise to new ways of expressing the trilogy of colour, sex, and sin.

The most forceful new expression of these themes was William Shakespeare's play *Othello*. It is also a particularly useful example of the evolution of British racial beliefs because it was penned at the same time they were expanding their contacts with Africa.

Shakespeare's reversal of black and white as symbols of good and evil are at the centre of the play. The hero Othello is black but has a white soul, whereas the villain Iago is white, but has a black character. This contrast works so well dramatically because the original meanings and symbolism of the colours were etched in the audience's minds. The impact of Shakespeare's images upon his audiences, and his skillful weaving of highly emotional themes into the play, indicate their importance in the society for which he was writing.

At that very moment the British were encountering the peoples of West Africa. One of the lightest complexioned people in the world, with a profound colour bias anchored in the deepest levels of their personalities, suddenly met some of the darkest complexioned people in the world. In that brief historical moment were sown the seeds of centuries of brutality, bloodshed, and racial hatred. The echoes of that confrontation continue to roll across North America even now.

The historical attitude of the British toward blackness was a fundamental factor in their exploitation of Africa. In many British minds the dark-skinned peoples of Africa were obviously cursed. Initially, many Britons felt revulsion to what they perceived to be black-skinned people and tried to avoid contact with them, foreshadowing their later attempts at racial segregation around the world.

Nor did the British immediately begin enslaving the black people they encountered on their African voyages of discovery. The Spanish and Portuguese were initially far ahead of them in that brutal industry. Only when their newly established colonies in North America and the Caribbean began clamouring for labourers was the latent British racism activated, and they entered the slave trade in any substantial way. As the white-skinned servants of God the British felt justified in chaining and using Africans for the betterment of their own society.

A tragic irony of British history is that Britons became involved in the slave trade at all. Beginning with the Magna Carta there had been a sporadic but steady development of more individual rights and freedoms in Britain. It was a major reversal of its own evolution as a society for such a country to revert to an ancient legal and social institution such as slavery.

Still, the British did embrace slavery and, given their special genius for large-scale maritime enterprises, they soon dominated the cruel trade. The British, and their colonial offspring, were able to overcome the obvious contradiction between expanding individual rights and enslaving individuals because of the latent racism in their societies. For white Britons, and colonial Americans, Africans were not entitled to freedom because their colour proved that they were a lesser form of humanity.

Racism was thus not simply an excuse for enslaving Africans. Rather, it was the basis of an industry that brought thousands to North America in chains. In North America slavery was an expression of British and American racism that was triggered by economic demand.

Colonial Americans, especially those in the south, adopted slavery because it was both an economic system, and a means of racial control. In the minds of the white masters, the black slaves' colour was a badge of their racial inferiority and legitimized their use as chattels. Once established, the institution developed a ruthless logic of its own. The slaves' depressed condition, compared to the rest of colonial society, added to the idea that they were an inferior type of people. The longer African Americans were kept down, the more each generation of white southerners could feel that slavery was both right and proper. The natural conservatism of human institutions encouraged many southerners to accept and defend slavery as part of their way of life.

The southern colonies became the home of North American slavery because as thirteen of Britain's North American colonies evolved into the United States the institution both expanded and receded. By the eve of the Civil War, white planters from the south took slavery as far west as Texas. Meanwhile their northern countrymen got rid of the institution in every state in the north, and spread the free territory to the edge of the Great Plains as well as to the west coast. At the peak of its development in the United States, racial slavery was peculiarly a southern institution.

There were several reasons why whites living in the northern states abolished slavery. The main factor was that it was simply of little use to them economically. Another element was the growth of powerful groups dedicated to ending slavery. Ironically, one of the main reasons for the success of the abolitionists was the racism of their audiences. Slavery meant African Americans, and most whites living in the north and mid-west of the United States did not want blacks living in their communities. The treatment of free blacks in northern cities and in the mid-west, where segregation and discrimination were widespread, was designed to stop African Americans from migrating or fleeing there on their own. By opposing slavery's expansion westward the anti-slavery forces were trying to ensure that there would be few blacks on the western frontier. The bloody confrontation in Kansas in the 1850s over whether that state was to be slave or free was also a fight about the future colour of the Great Plains. After the turn of the century that fight would be resurrected in Oklahoma and on the Canadian Plains when African Americans tried moving to those areas.

The clash in Kansas was also an indication that the opposing sides on the slavery question were moving even further apart. Northerners and Westerners were determined that slavery would not expand. Southerners were equally insistent that they be allowed to take their human property anywhere they chose. The slave-owners also argued that they be allowed to re-capture slaves who had fled to the free states. Pressured by the slave states, the United States federal government passed a Fugitive Slave Act in 1850 permitting slaveowners or their agents to arrest escaped slaves in the free states, and to transport them south. This law was bitterly opposed by both black and white abolitionists, some of whom organized the now famous Underground Railroad to help the slaves escape again — to Canada.

British law, which had forbidden slavery since 1834, protected these African Americans when they fled northward in the 1850s. After the American Revolution the British colonies in North America only united to form the country of Canada in 1867. Until that time they were subject to the laws of the mother country, and were therefore free territory for the former American slaves.

Not that these refugees from the Fugitive Slave Act were the first people of African descent in what was to become Canada. Black is one of the oldest colours in the Canadian mosaic. There had been African slaves in Quebec since at least 1632. British officers stationed in the former French colony after the conquest of 1760 also had black servants. American slave owners who had stayed loyal to their King brought their chattels with them when they fled north after the American Revolution. Many of these people settled in the then colonies of Nova Scotia and New Brunswick. There were also black Loyalists or Tories, depending on which side you fought, particularly from the southern colonies, who had fled to the British lines during the Revolutionary War, and fought their former masters for their own freedom. These African Americans were given land in Nova Scotia, where many of their descendants still live.

The absence of slavery after British abolition did not mean that there was no racial prejudice in what was to become Canada. As descendants of European Christians, many with British roots, Canadians had definite views on blackness and dark-skinned peoples, and these were generally hostile. The Canadian admission of escaped slaves prior to the American Civil War is often touted as an example of racial tolerance, but the lives of African Americans once in Canada were, in fact, far from ideal. Blacks were subjected to economic and social discrimination imposed by a racially conscious society. At one time, for example, both Ontario and Nova Scotia legislated separate schools for people of African ancestry.

The African Americans who fled to Canada in the 1850s found freedom, but not the racial haven they were seeking. Perhaps the best indicator of their disillusionment was that most of them returned to their native country during and after the American Civil War. Still, some did stay, particularly in southwestern Ontario, where their descendants still reside.

Flight to Canada was only one example of the most common protest against slavery. African-American slaves resisted the institution which bound them by fleeing from it. Running away was so common during the entire history of American slavery that it could be seen as a characteristic of the institution. There were many other ways of resisting slavery. These ranged from work slow downs to arson and murder. There were also several outright rebellions, although these tended to be localized, and were quickly crushed.

Even though there had only been a few slave rebellions southern whites feared one when the Civil War erupted. Still, there was no rising between 1861 and 1865, leading some whites to claim that the slaves were docile and happy with their lot in life. The truth was probably that the bondsmen were biding their time, waiting for an opportunity to be free.

A main reason why the slaves did not rebel during the war was that they had to contend with increased white vigilance and repression. That the white South was at war did not mean that it was unable to maintain its slave control system. In many areas extra precautions were taken, white boys and older men were pressed into service, and white women took on new responsibilities. In addition, as President Lincoln himself recognized, the fact that Southern society was organized militarily meant that it would be easier to crush any uprising of unarmed slaves.

Nor did slave control always wear the grey uniform of the southern Confederacy. Several blue-coated generals of the Union forces let it be known that they would use their troops to quash any slave rebellion. In the early stages of the war it was also not uncommon for Union troops to return runaway slaves to their masters.

The slaves knew about these Union army policies, and saw the increased southern control every day. The slaves appear to have sensibly adopted a "wait and see" attitude, and went on working. It was obviously foolish to rebel if even the northern troops would fight you.

Just as before the war, the most popular way to become free was with your feet. Now, however, there were many more opportunities. No sooner did Union troops enter an area in the south than they were confronted with hundreds of runaways. At first these slaves were turned away, or returned to their masters. But there were so many runaways that new policies evolved, and blacks began to be used on non-combatant army jobs. Having tasted liberty these freedmen, as they came to be called, and other free blacks insisted on their right to fight for the freedom of their brethren. Eventually black regiments were organized, commanded by white officers, and by the end of the war one of every ten men wearing a blue uniform had a black complexion.

Once underway the use of these troops spread rapidly, as did the white southern fear of them. African-American troops sent a shudder through the southern Confederacy because they represented the spectre of a black over white society, with all of the sexual and religious connotations of that image. The white South responded by declaring these soldiers to be outlaws who, if captured, could be executed for taking part in a slave rebellion.

Many white southerners had gone to war because they feared a future where slavery was limited. Many continued to fight because they feared a future without slavery. These people were also subjected to pounding wartime propaganda, from the Confederate government and southern newspapers, which accentuated their fear. This fear was increased many times over with the defeat of the Confederate armies. Still reeling from that defeat southern whites suddenly had to confront the realization that they did not know their former bondsmen as well as they had thought they did.

Their racism had led southern whites to believe that their slaves had an instilled spirit of obedience. The newly freed blacks now left their old homes, and often paid no heed to their former masters or to any whites. Shocked southern whites began to understand that their image of "Sambo," the old faithful black servant, was a myth. Southern whites had believed this myth, had drawn comfort from it, and its removal only added to their fear of the future.

Fearful of a future in which blacks were unchained, with all that that implied, southern whites fell back on the certainty of their racism. Since they could not accept African Americans as anything but their inferiors, they began to search for a new form of obedience among their former bondsmen. When whites did not find the behaviour they wanted among blacks, they created it — with force. Violence and intimidation were aimed at the freedmen as the white south tried to make "Sambo" a reality. Slavery may have been abolished in the United States, but its legacy was the colour caste system of the American south.

The white South needed black obedience to overcome its fear, and to confirm its racist views. This ran counter to the new needs of the blacks themselves. Freed from the chains of slavery, African Americans wanted the benefits of freedom.

If liberty were their goal during slavery, then owning land became the African American aim afterward. Their land hunger derived from several sources. After the Civil War most African Americans were rural peasants, and land hunger is a characteristic of any peasantry regardless of their colour. Another source of land hunger was the African Americans' acculturation: the individual ownership of property is one of the foundations of American society. Another part of the land hunger came from the blacks' sense of justice. Black hands had cleared, drained, sown, and harvested much of the south's agricultural land. In many African-American minds it was only fair that the land belonging to supporters of the Confederacy be turned over to them.

African-American land hunger following the Civil War came to be focused upon the idea of a general division of property among the former bondsmen. This notion may have originated in Union army experiments during the war in which confiscated lands in Union-controlled areas of the south were subdivided and farmed by newly freed blacks. The idea took root with freedmen that these policies would continue, and that each of them would receive "forty acres and a mule." This belief became widespread among African Americans after the war. Northern travellers in the south at the time rarely failed to comment on how many blacks thought that they would be getting land. The idea of a property division became so strong that the United States federal government had to issue a public letter denying it, and had the letter widely distributed.

Of course white Southerners did not want to give up their land. Even though they had been defeated in the war some of them were prepared to fight again if their land was taken from them. As always their anxiety led to fears of a black rebellion, and steps were taken to counter what many whites saw as a potential threat. Patrols and militia companies were organized across the South. African Americans were warned by white spokesmen that if they used force to obtain land it would be met with force, and that any violence on their part would be dealt with quickly.

African Americans knew that land would give them the foundation they needed to build new lives. It would be a base upon which all of their new freedoms would rest. White Southerners were determined to keep the land they held. They also wanted a quiet, obedient labour force to work that land. A confrontation between these black and white positions loomed, and the decades following the Civil War witnessed bloody attempts to resolve it.

The Klu Klux Klan was the white South's most infamous weapon in this racial struggle. The Klan built on the south's long tradition of night riding to keep the slaves under control. Slave patrols had existed until the end of the Civil War, and it took little effort to revive them in a new disguise.

Founded in Tennessee in 1865 as an adventure-seeking fraternal organization the Klan grew rapidly after the war. The companionship and regalia attracted many recruits, but the main reason for the Klan's popularity among whites was its ability to terrorize the former slaves, or whites who sided with them. African Americans who questioned or challenged the prevailing ideas of white supremacy could expect a visit from the Klan. Blacks who became too prosperous for their white neighbours' liking would find the white-robed riders at their door. The Klan intimidated by burning symbols and property, and by physical — sometimes fatal — violence. The black victims of the shooting, lynching, and running-off were frequently the leaders of their communities. Their removal deprived African Americans of much needed guidance to mount an effective resistance.

The violence of the Klan and other similar groups pressed African Americans into defined social and economic roles, and legislation was passed to keep them there. Before the Civil War, masters and slaves had shared all manner of public facilities. Such familiarity was no longer acceptable to a majority of whites once the blacks were freed, and increasingly the two races were kept apart.

Racial segregation in public services had actually first developed in the northern and mid-western states as a way of discouraging free blacks or escaped slaves from moving to those areas. These practices migrated south after the Civil War where they became an entrenched part of southern society. As early as 1866 Texas tried to segregate African Americans on railroad trains. It was another decade before a fairly well established system of segregation was in operation. The name given to these practices was "Jim Crow," the name of a black character in a popular minstrel show, and in the following years the southern states moved to make such segregation the law.

African Americans never accepted these infringements on their rights, and in every decade from their implementation there were protests and legal challenges. The black community suffered a major set-back in such efforts when in 1896 the United States Supreme Court confirmed the validity of racial segregation laws. It was the civil rights movement of the 1950s and 1960s which finally began to overturn this legal segregation.

During this segregation era, southern state legislatures also moved to stop African Americans from voting. African Americans had gained the ballot with the Fifteenth Amendment to the United States Constitution. Many southern whites, who overwhelmingly supported the Democratic Party, expected blacks to vote as they were instructed. These whites were shocked and angered when blacks voted for Lincoln's party, the Republicans. Slavery had kept many African Americans ignorant and illiterate but it had not made them foolish, and they supported the party which had fought for their freedom.

The southern states did not move as quickly to disfranchise black voters as they did to segregate them. The Fifteenth Amendment was a major, and powerful, obstacle to anyone who thought about making voting a "whites only" exercise. Also, in some areas of the south, letting blacks vote for the Republicans was a way for the Democrats to ensure that white racists would continue to vote for them. In other areas of the region alliances could be made with black politicians, supported by black votes, to back one white political faction against another. All of these factors worked against disfranchisement, and it was not until 1890 that the state of Mississippi led the way in taking the ballot out of black hands.

The men who influenced Mississippi politics disfranchised the African-American voters of the state because they had been frightened by developments at the national level. In 1888 both the federal House of Representatives and the Senate had been captured by the Republicans. Southern white Democrats were concerned about what their political enemies would do with their new-found power. They did not have to wait long to find out. In 1890 Congress passed the so called "Lodge Force Bill" which provided for federal election supervision. If federal election officials began to check national election returns, then the corrupt voting practices which kept white Democrats in power in the South might disappear, with the frightening prospect of an increase in power for southern Republicans and their black supporters.

Mississippi proposed to deal with this problem by eliminating African Americans from politics altogether. In other southern states white Democrats turned to Mississippi to learn how to eliminate the threatening black ballots.

In the American system of government each state has its own constitution, not just the country as a whole. Periodically these documents need to be revised and updated, and a constitutional convention is held to write a new one. Mississippi took advantage of this opportunity and, in a new state constitution, outlined a variety of techniques to limit African American voting.

Having only recently left slavery most southern blacks were poor, and their poverty was the target of poll tax and property requirements for voting in the new Mississippi Constitution. Poor people tend to move frequently looking for work, and Mississippi tightened residency requirements for casting ballots. African Americans also had a relatively high illiteracy rate at this time because slavery had deprived them of even a basic education. This weakness in the black community was the target of tests which required voters to be able to read and write to the satisfaction of an election supervisor, or be able to understand material read to them.

There was a problem with these voting restrictions. All of them could also be used against poor whites, many of whom cast their ballots for the Democrats. Since it was the Democrats who were making these changes they did not want to upset one of their own constituencies.

The problem of the poor white voter was dealt with by a "Grandfather Clause" in the new Mississippi Constitution. The clause took its name from its provision that none of the franchise restrictions applied if you or one of your ancestors had voted before 1861. Since most blacks had been slaves, and even free African Americans could not vote before that date, the Grandfather Clause effectively allowed poor whites to continue voting while excluding blacks.

Campaigns to segregate and disfranchise African Americans in the south were aided by the rising international tide of "scientific" racism in the late nineteenth century. White American and European scientists had used their knowledge to propose racist doctrines in the past, but had based their ideas on theories outmoded by Charles Darwin. This new variety of racism used Darwinian precepts to develop theories of human development which invariably placed non-whites lower on an evolutionary scale than whites.

Darwin had himself been a firm abolitionist, and downplayed attempts to apply his biological theories to society. It was left to his countryman Herbert Spencer to develop a coherent social philosophy based upon Darwinian ideas for the British, coining the immortal phrase "survival of the fittest" in the process. Spencer's adaptation became widely known in North America, and in the United States was discussed alongside the work of their own William Graham Sumner. Sumner was an influential sociologist who had similarly developed a theory of society based upon Darwinian ideas of evolution. Sumner and Spencer in turn laid the groundwork for such later popular racist writers as Lothrop Stoddard, author of *The Rising Tide of Colour Against White World Supremacy*, and Maidson Grant, a lawyer and author of *The Passing of the Great Race*.

African Americans did not simply accept these attacks upon their humanity, or their democratic rights. They organized and fought the Ku Klux Klan, although the battle was one-sided because southern whites had greater firepower and superior numbers. African Americans demonstrated against segregation, launched boycotts, and protested individually. These activities were usually met with indifference, and often hostility. African Americans also took their pleas to court, but met with little justice there.

The failure of African Americans to get help from their nation's courts in their struggle with segregation and disfranchisement was an indication of the depth of the racism which they faced. The United States had inherited the British commitment to greater individual rights and freedoms, breaking with their mother country when the evolution of those ideas appeared to be stalled. Still, for all of their reverence for liberty, throughout most of their history white citizens of the United States have been unwilling and unable to share those rights with their nation's black minority. The reason for this discrimination has been white racism.

White racism is a twisted, complex set of emotions and beliefs. Anchored in the way a people view themselves, express themselves, and communicate their religious ideas, it has been transformed by secular attitudes and "scientific" theories. Yet it has never lost its core belief — that one people is superior to another because of biological inheritance.

Racism was another part of North America's British inheritance, and until recently it has proven to be more powerful than constitutional legalisms. White North Americans, whether of British ancestry or assimilated into the dominant society, have acquired a powerful bias against blackness, and dark-skinned peoples. In the United States the experience with racial slavery had built upon these basic ideas to create the overwhelming conviction among white Americans that they were racially superior to their black fellow citizens. Believing that they were the superior race white Americans, particularly those in the South, felt justified in granting or removing democratic rights from what they believed to be an inferior type of people.

African Americans would not accept the idea that they were inferior. They fought the idea and its legal and social consequences. African Americans died in their efforts to gain equality. Others were defeated in the struggle by greater numbers and intense racial hatred. Still others followed the example of their slave ancestors, and fled for freedom rather than accept a new form of bondage. One of their destinations was the Indian Territory — the future state of Oklahoma. When Oklahoma began to implement racial segregation and disfranchisement small groups of black settlers headed north to Canada, only to face the racist virus again.

Chapter Two

RACISM MIGRATES WESTWARD

Whenever a 'Creek negro' (Nigger is the general term used) gets liquor he usually wants to start trouble. He is vicious. The Indian blood does not seem to elevate the negro, but it puts the Indian fight into him and it crops out just as soon as he gets drunk...
— Oklahoma City *Daily Oklahoman,*
26 January 1907.

T he huge interior plain of North America rises at the Gulf of Mexico, west of the Mississippi delta, and heads north for its rendezvous with the northern lights. Narrow at the base, it gradually widens to touch mountains on the west, and river valleys feeding the Mississippi on the east. Just north of Texas, where the southern plain touches the valleys, a racial drama unfolded whose echoes would rebound to its northern limits.

Where valley and plain meet was once known as the Indian Territory, set aside by the United States federal government as a place to settle aboriginal nations removed from the path of advancing white settlement. Both black and white settlers eventually moved into the Indian Territory, and together with the aboriginal inhabitants created a unique and volatile racial situation.

In the 1820s and 1830s the expanding republic forced several thousand members of the Creek (Muskogee), Cherokee, and Choctaw Nations to leave their lands in the Carolinas, Alabama, and Tennessee. They were given new homelands across the Mississippi, and promises that this land would always belong to

19

them. They were joined in the Indian Territory by the Chickasaws and Seminoles from Mississippi and Florida. These nations had adopted many white practices, and when they were moved west whites called them the "Five Civilized Tribes" to set them apart from the Plains peoples.

One of the white institutions these nations had accepted was racial slavery, and it was well established among them when they were herded west. Indeed, many of the migrants on what became known as the "Trail of Tears" were black slaves. The treatment of these slaves varied from nation to nation. Creeks and Seminoles married African Americans, and the children of such unions were recognized as members of the nations. The Cherokees were against such racial mixing while the Choctaws were known to be firmly against the abolition of the institution of slavery.

It is not surprising that there was a strong pro-Confederate feeling among the aboriginals when the Civil War began. Such sympathies were not universal and, like the rest of the country, the Five Civilized Tribes were divided by the war. Guerrilla warfare between opposing factions in the Indian Territory took a heavy toll.

Officially these aboriginal nations remained loyal to the United States. After the war the American federal government nevertheless accused the nations of rebellion, and dictated terms of surrender. Black slaves were the focus of two provisions of the post-war treaties. Slavery was abolished, and the former bondsmen were to become members of the nations.

The Creeks and Seminoles had little trouble dealing with these terms of the treaties because they had already accepted blacks into their nations. Not so with the Chickasaws and the Choctaws. At first they refused to give up their slaves unless they were compensated for them. One leader threatened to round up all of his nation's slaves and herd them to Texas unless compensation was forthcoming.

The Cherokees were also bitter with the treaty provisions, but focused their anger on another clause, one giving former slaves held by the Five Civilized Tribes six months to register to become members of the aboriginal nations. The Cherokees, and members of other nations, feared that African Americans who had never even seen the Indian Territory would move there, claim tribal membership, and obtain a share of the land. While such disputes were eventually settled they left a legacy of bitterness toward African Americans among some of the aboriginals.

This ill will continued for years because African Americans living in states bordering the Indian Territory were indeed attracted by the opportunity to obtain aboriginal land. Prospective black settlers were also encouraged to move to the area by rumours, circulating in Washington, D.C., that Republicans in Congress were going to pass legislation allowing blacks other than former Indian slaves to settle upon the aboriginal lands.

This Congressional plan never did develop, but the rumour bolstered the widespread belief among African Americans that their federal government was going to give each of them "forty acres and a mule." Together, these rumours and ideas were enough to cause African Americans living in Texas, Arkansas, Missouri and other states in the region to move to the Indian Territory.

The black migration to the aboriginal lands began after the Civil War and continued into the 1880s. The movement was replenished by new rumours, such as one which had "eastern philanthropists" deciding to help African Americans obtain aboriginal land. These mysterious humanitarians were said to have decided that African Americans were the only citizens of the United States who had a right to settle upon ceded lands in the Indian Territory. This "right" was apparently based upon the post-war treaties' provisions regarding the former aboriginal slaves. According to one local source, "parties are now at work in earnest organizing colonies of coloured men to drop in on the promised land."

African-American migration to the Indian Territory was only part of a larger, steady stream of black settlers moving from the older southeastern states to the new lands of the west. In the decades following the Civil War thousands of African Americans joined their fellow white citizens in looking for opportunities on the frontier. They were driven by their desire for better wages, or better share-cropping contracts. Others were spurred by the violence of the Ku Klux Klan, and similar groups. Most clung to the dream of someday owning their own piece of land.

Some of these African Americans headed directly to the Indian Territory. Others moved to Kansas first, and only later migrated to what became the state of Oklahoma. In the late 1870s thousands of African Americans headed to Kansas when they heard glowing reports about that state. Many white southerners and Democrats saw the movement as a Republican plot to reinforce their voting strength in the mid-west. Other white southerners, fearful of losing their labour supply, tried to stop the flow with a variety of brutal techniques.

For many African Americans the idea of settling in Kansas was not a new one. That state had once been suggested as a refuge for discharged black Union soldiers who could not return to their southern homes for fear of white vengeance. African Americans living in Tennessee and neighbouring states had also heard about Kansas from Benjamin "Pap" Singleton, who encouraged settlement in the western state as the only hope for his people. African Americans in many parts of the south were given the "word" by this self-styled "Moses of the Colored Exodus," and the word was "land." Between five and ten thousand black settlers actually moved to Kansas, and many more would likely have followed if the stories about Kansas had remained favourable.

Kansas was not the utopia these African American settlers were seeking. Most of the "exodusters," as they were called, arrived penniless, and just before the onslaught of winter. Tales of misery and poverty returned to the places of departure with disillusioned settlers, and by 1881 the black migration to Kansas was in its death throes.

Still, the ideas of land and liberty were interconnected in many African-American minds, and would not die easily. During the 1880s they were resurrected as more African Americans looked toward the Indian Territory. "Pap" Singleton, who as a slave had escaped to Canada, did not give up on his idea of a black Canaan. He tried to create interest in a movement to Canada, but met with little success. When the future state of Oklahoma did not become the new black utopia, African Americans were to look north after all.

African Americans who remained in Kansas after the migration found that they had to move to the towns and cities in order to survive. Some of them prospered, but for most black Kansans the biggest change in their situation was their political status. The Kansas Republicans began courting the new black voters. African-American voters quickly exercised their new influence. In 1882 they helped to elect a black man, Edward P. McCabe, as Kansas state auditor on the Republican ticket.

The African-American political success in Kansas was all too brief. By the mid-1880s the Kansas Republicans had become indifferent to the black voters, and dumped McCabe. The Republicans instead turned their efforts toward recruiting the white immigrants who were arriving in the state in large numbers. There was also a notable rise in racial feeling in Kansas, with several bloody racial clashes, including lynchings.

Many Kansas blacks came to believe that without political power they were defenceless against white racism. Some African-American voters turned to the Kansas Peoples' Party, or Populists, which was beginning to organize. Other African Americans, including E.P. McCabe, felt that the only way to gain liberty-giving political power was to create a state that they would control. It was evident that the Indian Territory would soon become a state, and McCabe began encouraging Kansas blacks to move south so that an African-American majority might be reached in each voting district.

The idea of a black state evaporated in the racial heat of the southern plains. The white settlers pouring into the Indian Territory were not going to let it happen, and neither was the United States federal government. McCabe did not give up his idea and for some time continued to urge his fellow African Americans to migrate to the Indian lands. He founded a newspaper that promoted the virtues of aboriginal land, and he became involved with a land development project at Langston, Indian Territory. He also started a company whose agents went across the southern states carrying his newspaper and preaching another African-American migration westward.

McCabe's efforts attracted more black settlers to the Indian Territory, but not enough to ensure a black-controlled state. In fact, when Oklahoma was organized it was predominantly white, and moved quickly to implement the racist policies of the older southern states. McCabe then, like a number of African Americans in Oklahoma at the time, looked northward for an escape. In 1908 the former Kansas auditor and Oklahoma promoter moved to Victoria, British Columbia, Canada.

Many more whites than blacks were heading to the aboriginal lands because there was property to be had, particularly after the United States federal government responded to the increasing pressure for settlement. The nations of the Indian Territory held their land communally, not individually. As always, prospective settlers felt that the aboriginals had too much land and they were not using it efficiently. The settlers and land promoters put pressure on the American federal government to make more land available for settlement. They were successful, and in 1887 Congress passed the Dawes Act which reneged on earlier promises to the aboriginals that their land would always belong to them.

The new legislation ended the nations' communal holdings, with devastating results to their societies. It also allotted each member of a nation the title to a homestead. The remaining land was purchased by the federal government, and opened to settlement. Initially the Dawes Act only applied to other aboriginal nations which had been moved to the Indian Territory, and not to the Five Civilized Tribes. In 1896, however, the act was extended to include them as well.

Land which had not been allotted to the aboriginal nations was also opened for settlement, and was the goal of those taking part in the now famous Oklahoma "land rushes." Settlers swarmed over the western section, or Oklahoma district, of the Indian Territory. Between 1889 and 1900 over sixty thousand farms were developed on what had been virtual wilderness. It became apparent that a new government structure was required, and in 1890 the Territory of Oklahoma was separated from the older Indian Territory to the east. Settlers also infiltrated the lands of the Five Civilized Tribes and the other nations inhabiting what was left of the Indian Territory. By 1890 the Cherokees, Choctaws, and Chickasaws were minorities in their own nations. The Creeks, meanwhile, were able to maintain only a bare majority.

The first settlers in what became the Oklahoma Territory immediately began to agitate for statehood. Their demands had been anticipated in Congress, and in 1889 a bill had been introduced in the House of Representatives which would have admitted part of the Indian Territory into the American union as the state of Columbia. This legislation died because the Democrats and Republicans in Congress were at odds over the admission of new states from the southwest. The Republicans felt that the Oklahoma and Indian Territories should be admitted as one state, as should New Mexico and Arizona, since they would all probably be Democratic in sympathy. Southern Democrats in particular wanted four separate states to be created so as to balance the new states created in the northwest.

The residents of the Twin Territories, as the Oklahoma and Indian Territories came to be called, were themselves badly divided on the issue. Republicans in the Oklahoma Territory felt that their national leaders were wrong, and that while the Indian Territory would probably go to the Democrats they could carry a

The United States with the State of
Oklahoma indicated.

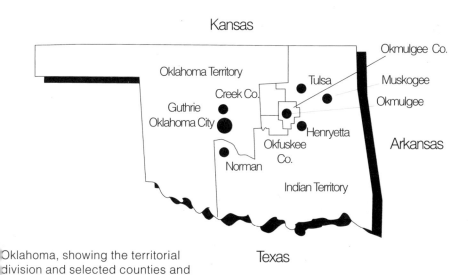

Oklahoma, showing the territorial
division and selected counties and
cities.

separate Oklahoma. Indian Territory Democrats were concerned that the already organized Oklahoma Territory would dominate any joint arrangement. Members of the Five Civilized Tribes feared that if they were grafted onto the Oklahoma Territory they would lose their identity in a sea of white faces.

This already complex political situation was made even more complicated when Congress passed the Curtis Act in 1898. This legislation terminated all of the aboriginal governments in the Indian Territory on 4 March 1906. This meant that the Indian Territory would have to organize along regular territorial lines like the Oklahoma Territory, or become a state.

In an attempt at statehood, a call for representatives was sent to each of the Five Civilized Tribes to meet in Muskogee beginning 21 August 1905. At this gathering a three thousand, five hundred word constitution was drafted which provided for universal suffrage, but separate schools for blacks. The "Sequoyah Constitution," as it was called, was submitted to the people of the Indian Territory, and they approved it by a vote of 56,279 to 9,073. A delegation took the document to Washington, and bills for statehood were introduced in both Houses of Congress.

But the prevailing sentiment in Congress had shifted yet again. A majority of legislators now favoured single statehood for the Oklahoma and Indian Territories, and the Sequoyah Constitution did not accomplish its task of making the Indian Territory into a separate state. The gathering at Muskogee did have important consequences for the future state, though, because it gave a number of aboriginal and white delegates invaluable political experience. It gave the Texan "Alfalfa Bill" Murray a priceless baptism in running a convention which paid dividends for him when the Oklahoma Constitutional Convention was eventually called. In addition, the gathering brought together Murray and Charles N. Haskell, a white delegate for the Creek Nation, and they cemented a political partnership which was to last through Haskell's term as the first Governor of the new state.

The Sequoyah Constitution, and its approval by the vast majority of Indian Territory citizens, also sent a message to African Americans living in the area. The proposal to legalize separate schools for black children was an ominous sign. The Oklahoma and Indian Territories were federally administered, and African Americans therefore had some protection in the exercise of their citizenship, but

Sequoyah illustrated all to clearly what would happen when local authorities took control of the levers of government.

African Americans had reason to be concerned. The white settlers invading the aboriginal lands brought a noticeable southern flavour to what would become Oklahoma. Of the more than one million white Oklahomans who claimed another state as their place of birth in the first census following statehood, fully one third were from Texas, Missouri, or Arkansas. The next largest group was from Kansas, and by the time of the census they had contributed almost seven percent of the white population. Political alignments in what became Oklahoma reflected this settlement pattern. The northern third of the future state favoured the Republicans, reflecting its proximity to Kansas. The central portion was moderately Democrat in sympathy, while the southern third of the new state would be dominantly Democrat.

The presence of a sizeable white Republican minority had important repercussions for African Americans in the area. This white Republican vote, combined with the traditional African-American allegiance to Lincoln's party, gave white Democrats constant cause for concern. Ultimately it was to lead the Democrats to take away African-American voting rights, sending several hundred north to Canada.

Whatever their political leanings many white Americans did not want African Americans living near them. African-American settlers who had responded to the appeals of Edward McCabe met with violence and intimidation at the start of the 1889 "land rush." White newspapers in both the Indian and Oklahoma Territories had downplayed McCabe's efforts to create a black state, but some whites were prepared to take more direct action.

During the 1890s, there was racially motivated mob violence in both of the Territories. White communities would often band together to drive their African-American neighbours out of town. In Blackwell and Ponca City, towns along the northern border with Kansas, African Americans were hounded and driven out. White-robed riders made an appearance in Norman, in the centre of the future state, in 1896. These riders also appeared in other areas in subsequent years. All of these groups tried to drive African Americans out of their communities with whippings or beatings, and by threatening whites who employed blacks or rented land to them.

In 1901 the white residents of Sapulpa gave the town's African American population two days warning, and then drove them out. In the town of Clinton, notices were posted threatening the owners of a cotton seed mill which employed African Americans. Racial slurs were also part of the intimidation. An African-American doctor who went to Muskogee to write his medical examinations was told to "play nigger" by the head of the examining board. The doctor had to be forcibly restrained from attacking the examiner. How well he did on his examinations was not recorded.

Even economic necessity could not overcome some racial attitudes. When the 1905 Greer County cotton crop was threatened by a shortage of pickers, one hundred and fifty black workers were brought in to help save it. No African Americans had ever been allowed to live in the area, and this influx was resisted by some local whites making serious threats in an attempt to scare the workers away. Local officials had to warn those making the threats that action would be taken, and only then did the county become peaceful. In other areas African Americans could not even get jobs in the cotton fields. That same year the residents of Hobart voted not to employ African Americans that season, even for a short time.

African Americans protested the economic war which was being waged upon them. Most African-American settlers had come to the Oklahoma and Indian Territories hoping to better themselves. Their frustration at encountering the same racial economics which they had moved to escape was voiced by one black journalist when he complained:

> Of all the grievances that distress ambitious Negroes the most galling is the disadvantage of their own race in the matters of earning a living. None but menial positions are open to the black man, they say.

African-American settlers in what became Oklahoma also discovered that they had to contend with the ancient spectre of the "black rapist beast." Editors of African-American newspapers called attention to the problem, and repeatedly challenged the traditional image of black males. One African-American newspaperman argued that no one would defend a white woman faster than a black man, and noted as proof instances during the Civil War. He suggested that it was the image of his own sins that haunted the white man because it was he who had raped helpless African-American women under the noses of his own wife and daughter.

Another African-American editor wanted to know why outrages on black women by white men were not handled the same way as the reverse.

The spectre of interracial sex was also behind the white demand for racially segregated schools. In an era when many people found their future mates at school this issue generated the most racial controversy prior to statehood. In the Oklahoma Territory a bitter debate on the question developed in the legislature, and segregationists successfully carried a bill which provided for local option.

All of the Five Civilized Tribes had segregated school systems, but the influx of racially opinionated whites hardened attitudes considerably. In the Creek Nation it had not been uncommon for black children to attend the regular schools. By 1904, however, citizen and non-citizen blacks were required to attend the separate schools.

African Americans living in the Indian Territory protested this development claiming that southern sentiments were overcoming the western spirit of fair play. In a rare display of reverse prejudice a black editor claimed that the aboriginals were getting a bad deal sending their children to school with the offspring of "poor white trash." In his opinion such white youngsters were...

> mean and overbearing, they lie and use all kinds of bad language, at home and at school; they are filthy of their person and many of them would wade through hell to steal a dinner pail with one biscuit in it. What they add to civilization don't count for much....

A white newspaper took up these comments, and angrily charged its black counterpart with being scurrilous. The black newspaper was on dangerous ground abusing the white man's children, even those of the lower classes, it argued. In a later issue the same white newspaper told the black journal to take a broader view of the issue. It was a universal human trait for the strong to oppress the weak, it said, and not simply a characteristic of the white race.

African Americans did not tamely submit to these developments in the school systems. One group of African-American parents went to court against their local school board for not allowing their children into the public schools. They were temporarily successful because as long as the Indian and Oklahoma Territories held territorial status they were subject to American federal jurisdiction.

Still, African Americans faced formidable opposition on the issue of segregated schools. Even their political allies, the Republicans, were against them on this question. One white Republican editor claimed that anyone who favoured mixed schools lacked ordinary sense. This journalist inadvertently revealed the pseudo-biological basis of racism by claiming that mankind was the only animal that wilfully broke nature's law against mixing the species. His opinion was that "Mixed schools breed contempt, jealousy, and race war."

As they had in other states and in other times, African Americans in the Twin Territories organized to protect themselves and to achieve their community's goals. Early in 1905 African-American teachers meeting at Guthrie, Oklahoma Territory, endorsed a resolution asking that all people be allowed uniformity in education. A call was issued in 1904 for the organization of an African-American Protection League, and in 1906 that newly formed group created an anti-lynching bureau.

Traditional organizations such as the church were also utilized in the struggle for justice. On 2 November 1906 the Oklahoma Conference of the African Methodist Episcopal Church passed a strongly worded anti-lynching statement. Churchmen, such as Parson H.L. Storms, who headed the African-American Independent Suffrage League, also played leading roles in secular organizations.

For some African Americans the best protection against white racism and its consequences was still in political numbers. One black newspaper urged its fellow African Americans to move to the town where it was published. That way, it argued, they would control the vote of an entire county before the inevitable arrival of statehood.

The flurry of organizational activity among African Americans prior to Oklahoma statehood indicates their concern. African Americans living in the Twin Territories desired their own local government as much as their fellow white citizens, but they also knew that unless they were organized they might well be drowned in a flood of racist legislation. African Americans knew the composition of the area's population, had dealt with white racism before, and had come from states where their rights had been infringed by the very documents which were supposed to protect them.

While some African Americans fought the entrenchment of white racial attitudes, or organized to protect their rights, others had had enough. The violence of the night riders, and the increasing discrimination based upon skin colour, was too much for some self-respecting blacks. In the Cherokee Nation the rise in racial feelings had added to other problems created by the influx of settlers. Conditions became so bad that a local black leader convinced almost eighty of his followers to head for Liberia in Africa. The potential colonists were both "black-Indians," and African Americans who had settled in the area. They were also highly agitated, and sold their land for small sums despite the prevailing high prices. Upon arriving in New York they discovered that their supposed leader had tricked them in order to obtain their land. They stayed in New York, along with other Africa-bound blacks from Arkansas, hoping something would develop which would help them on their way. Their ultimate fate remains unknown.

African Americans leaving the Oklahoma and Indian Territories passed others on the roads who could not wait to get to the Twin Territories. As bad as conditions were becoming for African Americans on the western plains they appeared to be better than in other southern states. The opportunity to obtain land, to get a base upon which to build a future, was too much for many to resist even though racial attitudes were hardening against them.

When in 1896 the Dawes Act was extended to include the Five Civilized Tribes black members of these nations were included in the land dispersal. This attracted the attention of African Americans living in nearby states. In 1898 Congress was told that there was likely to be another black influx into the Indian Territory. It was suggested that the movement would reach "alarming proportions" because small towns in Texas were organizing to drive out their African-American citizens. One local source suggested that the renewed migration was already underway: "The negroes were coming here by hundreds, lots of them thinking they, too, like the Indian freedmen, can get lands free for homes from the government."

African-American homeseekers often headed toward areas in the Indian Territory which were exclusively black. E.P. McCabe's dream of a black state had evaporated, but black newspapers promoted the idea of all-black districts. Towns which were all-black, and which served all-black or predominantly black rural areas were developed, at one point reaching more than two dozen in number.

The "black towns" illustrated the old adage of safety in numbers. They were also based upon a growing belief among some African Americans that the only way that they could control their own lives was away from the white majority. This self-segregation was heartily endorsed by whites who sometimes helped to develop such a town.

One example of the process was the town of Boley, an all-black community that was the idea of a white man, Lake Moore, President of the townsite division of the Fort Smith and Western Railway. Boley was launched in 1903, on the Fort Smith line, and within four years had over eight hundred residents. Boley trumpeted its success across the south, encouraging more African Americans to move to the Indian Territory. In its first issue the town's newspaper boasted,

> The Boley Progress makes its appearance in the interest of the long-felt necessity of furnishing homeseekers and colored capitalists of the states who require cheap homes and unrestrained privilege and paying investments, information pertaining to the many advantages possessed by Boley, Indian Territory — especially the Creek Nation.

While Boley welcomed newcomers to the area, the original inhabitants did not. Boley was located on land which had once belonged to former Creek Nation slaves. These "black-Indians" viewed the new African-American settlers as inferior. Racial attitudes were hardening as more white settlers arrived, and the "Creek-Negroes" blamed the "Watchina" or "State-Negroes" for their loss of social status. The Creek-Negroes felt that it was the black settlers who were to blame for the new racial system classifying the former aboriginal slaves as black, rather than as red.

The decline in the black-Indians' social standing had been particularly steep. The Creek-Negroes went from being full members of their nation to the lowest rung in the new white-dominated society. White racial attitudes toward these people were particularly harsh because they combined prejudice towards both blacks and aboriginals. How many whites viewed these people appears in the review of federal court records for the Creek and Choctaw Nations conducted by an influential white daily newspaper. According to this journal the largest number of murders and other serious crimes in these areas were committed by blacks with some aboriginal blood:

Whenever a `Creek negro' (Nigger is the general term used) gets liquor he usually wants to start trouble. He is vicious. The Indian blood does not seem to elevate the negro, but it puts the Indian fight into him and it crops out just as soon as he gets drunk....

Such attitudes dominated white racial views, and were the real source of the friction between the "Creek-Negroes" and the "Watchina." The tension kept the two groups apart and prevented them from cooperating to fight the new racial code, or to leave together for a safe haven. Instead there was violent conflict. Boley was the scene of gun fights, with killings and woundings on both sides. While this violence eventually declined it left a legacy of bitterness and distrust between the two groups.

Despite these problems black towns such as Boley were initially able to attract more black settlers, and the Creek Nation came to be included in the future state's "black belt." Most of these African Americans obtained their land through the Indian allotments. For them it must have been the realization of a dream, and from the base the land provided they were able to develop considerable political power in defense of that dream.

The success of these settlers continued to attract more African Americans, and this was duly noted in the local white press. According to one such source the Creek Nation was full of blacks. This same journal also declared that, "This situation became generally known all over the south — advertised by Negro papers as the place where a black man had a chance. The result has been more Negroes."

These people sought land, and a racial haven in the west. Unfortunately for them when Oklahoma became a state it began to implement all of the racist legislation of a southern state, a development which sparked some African Americans to begin looking for another escape route.

Chapter Three

STATEHOOD AND SEGREGATION

I have a great respect for an ex-slave and he could get anything from me, but the young negro who would come to me on the basis of equality and ask me to set 'em up I should feel like hitting him over the head with a club."

— "Alfalfa Bill" Murray in
a speech accepting the
Presidency of the Oklahoma
Constitutional Convention,
November 1906

O n 20 November 1906 the delegates to the Oklahoma Constitutional Convention assembled in Guthrie, a town in the centre of the future state. In a ritual dating back to the founding of the American republic they set about creating a legal framework for a new state government. Their activities also began a process which sent hundreds of their black fellow citizens toward the Canadian Plains.

One of the delegates' first acts was to elect a President for their gathering. They chose William Murray of Tishomingo, a community near the southern border with Texas. "Alfalfa Bill," as he was called, was a Texan who had moved north to the old Indian Territory. He had practised law, but was better known as a promoter of new farming methods, an activity which had provided him with his colourful nickname. Murray was as agrarian in his political philosophy, and a bit of a populist. His belief in that strain of American democracy did not include African Americans, and in his speech accepting the Presidency of the Constitutional Convention he revealed the white racism which was at the centre of an economic and social struggle in the emerging state.

Murray told his fellow delegates:

> We should adopt a provision prohibiting the mixed marriages of negroes with other races in this State, and provide for separate schools and give the Legislature power to separate them in waiting rooms and on passenger coaches, and all other institutions of the state. We have no desire to do the negro an injustice. We shall protect him in his real rights...We must provide the means for the advancement of the negro race, and accept him as God gave him to us and use him for the good of society.

Murray's references to colour, religion and interracial sex were more than an attempt to arouse his fellow delegates to legislative action. They were also a forceful expression of the main elements of his racial beliefs, attitudes shared by other descendants of Anglo-Europeans across North America.

Under the American system of government, the people of a territory wishing to form a state first apply to the Congress. If Congress favours the admission it passes an enabling act, one condition of which is a state constitution. The territory then elects delegates to a constitutional convention to compose the document. The state constitution, once drafted, is voted on by the people of the proposed state and, if accepted, is sent to the President for his approval. With his agreement, the territory becomes a state, and holds an election to choose its state officers and legislature.

African Americans, refugees from the politics of racism, had moved west seeking land and liberty only to be caught once more in the web of white racism. Many of them had moved to the Twin Territories to escape the racism which had been entrenched in reformed state constitutions. Many African Americans had also had a taste of what to expect locally when the Sequoyah Constitution had proposed racially segregated schools. Their fellow white citizens now sought to extend to the new state the racial segregation system of the older southern states.

As early as 1905 African Americans in the Territories had organized a convention in Muskogee to promote statehood. Like their white neighbours they wanted a local government, but they also wanted to have blacks elected as delegates to the statehood convention. African Americans also made it clear that they wanted guarantees their voting rights would be protected, "Jim Crow" segregation would be forbidden, and that there would be no racially segregated schools.

The United States Congress approved the Oklahoma Enabling Act on 16 June 1906, and for the most part it met African-American demands. While one section of the act did allow for segregated schools, another stated that the Oklahoma Constitution should "make no distinction in civil or political rights on account of race or colour...." Defiantly ignoring this provision, the Democratic Party campaigned for Constitutional Convention delegates on the basis that they were the only party which white voters could trust to put segregated schools and other "Jim Crow" clauses in the new state Constitution.

A major weapon in the Democrats' campaign for delegates was the Oklahoma City newspaper the *Daily Oklahoman*. This journal boasted of a circulation approaching fourteen thousand five hundred in 1906, but actually reached many more people because small-town Democrat weeklies frequently reprinted its editorial comments. The Democrats' communication network was impressive: they could count upon nearly two hundred newspapers to carry their message in the two Territories.

The *Daily Oklahoman* was owned and edited by Roy E. Stafford, a native of Iowa who had lived in both Kansas and Colorado. He had taken part in the Cherokee Strip land rush, but had settled into journalism. One of many aggressive competitive white businessmen who had been lured to the Territories, he had bought and sold two smaller newspapers before purchasing the Democrats' flagship journal in 1900.

Stafford was known as a staunch Democrat. He was also a passionate racist, and used his newspaper to campaign for "Jim Crow" segregation in the new Constitution. Stafford constantly taunted the Republicans for their black following, and was not above invoking the ancient spectre of a black over white society. For example, when the Republicans held a nomination meeting attended by a large number of African Americans, Stafford's *Oklahoman* painted a "spectacle" of "black domination" with the black delegates "arrogantly" naming their own slate of candidates and "driving white men with the party lash."

Stafford's editorials provide an interesting insight into the Democrats' position on the segregation issue. According to this

Oklahoma journalist white passengers on the railroads and street cars were forced to suffer the indignity of either riding with blacks or standing up. The Republicans, he claimed, knew how whites felt about this matter but remained silent. According to the *Oklahoman* the Republican strategy was to convince African Americans that they would not enact any segregation legislation while at the same time giving whites the false belief that they too favoured "Jim Crow." Consequently, the Republicans ought not to be trusted to deal with the segregation issue.

On the issue of racial segregation in schools the *Oklahoman* was even more direct. After noting that the Democrats had pledged separate schools in the Oklahoma Territory, the journal declared:

> In all the districts where the politicians are running the party, the republicans have not declared for separate schools and separate coaches. They must have the negro vote to win... Summed up it is the old story. The Republican politician cannot be separated from the 'nigger.'

This message was well received across the Territories. White voters repeatedly contacted Stafford to indicate their support for a racial segregation system. Stafford used these letters to bolster his campaign, and reprinted them in the pages of the *Oklahoman*.

The Democrats' campaign for Constitutional Convention delegates was helped by conflicts within the Republican party. Party leaders were divided over whether the Twin Territories were ready for statehood. Unable to reach agreement they allowed their candidates to run independently, with no platform. The result was a very ineffective Republican campaign.

Despite the confusion in their political enemies' ranks the Democrats left little to chance. On election day the *Oklahoman* raised the old southern white fear of a black rebellion. Stafford's journal cited a Kansas newspaper which had urged African Americans in that state to arm themselves against losing their liberty as was happening in the Territories. According to the *Oklahoman*,

> Here is reflected pretty aptly the sentiment of the average negro. It shows that he is vigorously opposed to the democratic proposition of 'Jim Crow' laws, and is willing to use force, if need be, to prevent the enactment of the same.

The Democrats also used other tactics to try to limit the number of Republican votes. One of these, the affidavit system, was specifically aimed at black voters. A white Democrat would challenge the voting credentials of a black voter forcing the African American to obtain from one to four affidavits setting out his qualifications as a voter. Many African Americans could not afford the notary fees. Repeated challenges would discourage those who could, and they would leave the polls without voting.

The Democrats' campaign was effective, and they swept the election for Constitutional Convention delegates. Of the one hundred and twelve elected, fully ninety-six identified themselves as Democrats, and three others were Democrats in all but name. Most of the delegates were also originally from former slaveholding states.

The Democrats believed that their stand on "Jim Crow" segregation was the key to their victory. The *Oklahoman* gloated that the new state would soon become part of the "solid South." The journal also suggested that Texas was proud of Oklahomans because they had chosen its path on race relations, and not the one laid out in Kansas.

Other observers agreed on the importance of the race issue in the campaign, and also drew comparisons to Kansas and Texas. One commentator argued that:

> The negro question was paramount. Shall we have the negro giving people a Kansas dose of his ideas, or will we let him know that he is to be cared for as he is in Texas, was an idea which took form rather than expression. When put to the test the Republicans were as quick to give expression as were the Democrats.

The Oklahoma Constitutional Convention began in Guthrie in the Fall of 1906. The climate was particularly hostile to African Americans because only a few months earlier black troops stationed in Brownsville, Texas, had been involved in a disturbance in which one white man was killed and two others were wounded. There were several investigations, but it was concluded that while several of the soldiers were guilty their identities could not be determined because their comrades remained silent. As punishment President Theodore Roosevelt discharged the entire regiment without honour.

As white southerners the majority of the delegates in Guthrie already held strong views about African Americans. The Brownsville incident only added to their prejudice. When "Alfalfa Bill" Murray accepted the Presidency of the gathering, his acceptance speech posited that the President's dismissal of the black regiment was proof that African Americans were a failure as soldiers. They were also generally failures as doctors, lawyers, and in other professions, he argued. African Americans had to be taught for jobs they could handle, such as barbers, bootblacks, and porters. They could also be trained for jobs in agriculture, horticulture, and mechanics, Murray felt, but it should be obvious to everyone that African Americans could never rise to equal whites in the professions or become equal citizens dealing with public issues.

It was during this acceptance speech that Murray laid bare the core of his racial beliefs. Like Shakespeare's Iago he used the powerful image of interracial sex, and urged his fellow delegates to prohibit the marriages of African Americans with other races in the future state. Murray also wanted blacks to be segregated in all of the public facilities of the state so as to minimize contact between blacks and whites.

Such was the depth of his racism that Murray could claim that whites had no desire to be unjust to African Americans. Trying to balance his racism with his populist belief in individual rights Murray told the assembled delegates that they should protect the "real rights" of African Americans. What these were was never made clear, but it did mean accepting the fact that God had placed blacks on the earth, and that whites had a duty to help them improve and become of use to society.

Such blatant racism and patronizing attitudes were, of course, unacceptable to African Americans in the Territories, and they responded to the threat posed by the Constitutional Convention. They organized and petitioned for a State Constitution that would give equal rights to all people. When it was declared that the public galleries at the convention were to be segregated, and several thousand dollars were spent to construct new ones, African Americans responded by boycotting the sessions.

As emotionally forceful as they were it is doubtful that any of these African American protests were factors in the startling announcement by a Democratic Party leader that the new state could not have "Jim Crow" in its Constitution after all. Charles N. Haskell, Democratic floor leader at the Convention, had carefully examined all enabling acts which Congress had passed since the Civil War. He had discovered that all of them contained provisions prohibiting racial discrimination. Oklahoma's Enabling Act was no exception, and Haskell believed that President Theodore Roosevelt would reject the document, and thus postpone statehood, if it contained an article allowing segregation. Haskell proposed leaving segregation out of the Constitution entirely, arguing that the first State legislature could pass all of the necessary laws.

Charles Haskell was a native of Ohio, and was another of the ambitious, energetic white businessmen lured by its economic potential to what would become Oklahoma. He had arrived in Muskogee in 1901, and quickly emerged as one of that city's leading business leaders. He also became involved in politics, and was a delegate for the Creek Nation at the Sequoyah Constitution Convention where he had entered a political alliance with "Alfalfa Bill" Murray.

As a delegate to the Oklahoma Constitutional Convention, Haskell was known as a tenacious manipulator of opinion. He needed all of his persuasive skills on the "Jim Crow" issue since not more than a dozen of his fellow delegates agreed with him when he first pointed out the problem. Haskell set to work converting his associates, a formidable task since most of them had been elected on the Democrats' segregation platform. Haskell was able to delay a vote on the issue until he had opinion on his side, but it was not until the Democrats had held a third caucus that he had his majority.

Haskell won support for his position from a newspaper in Muskogee whose editor claimed it would be "impolitic" to include segregation in the Constitution. Roosevelt would probably reject the document if it contained a segregation clause. Why risk statehood if subsequent legislatures could provide all of the necessary laws?

Roy Stafford and his powerful *Oklahoman* opposed this interpretation. Stafford reminded the delegates that most of them had been elected on segregation pledges, and wondered whether Roosevelt had the right to refuse to accept their document. He urged the delegates to put segregation in the Constitution, and not leave it for the legislature.

Stafford and Haskell were already at odds. Stafford earlier and publicly had accused Haskell of rigging his election to the Constitutional Convention by arranging with Muskogee Republican leaders to have a black man run for delegate along with the regular white Republican candidate. The white man was persuaded to withdraw from the election, according to the *Oklahoman*, "leaving no one opposing him but the nigger. In that manner he slipped in."

Haskell counter-attacked vigorously. He accused the Oklahoma City daily of not being a true Democratic journal. It was also in the hands of "monopoly grafters," Haskell argued: a serious charge in an area with a radical agrarian history.

Haskell's position on the segregation issue was supported by several Democratic Senators in Washington. They felt that the President could very well reject the Oklahoma Constitution if it contained segregation clauses. Their reasoning was that Roosevelt had lost a good deal of black voter support because of the Brownsville affair, and he could rebuild his political fortunes among African-American voters in the north and mid-west by rejecting a "Jim Crowed" Oklahoma Constitution.

Some Oklahoma Democrats also recognized the problem they faced at the national level and, as one of them phrased it,

> There is no necessity of antagonizing the president on this subject and giving him an opportunity to make a grandstand play, which he surely would do, for the sole purpose of rehabilitating himself with the negroes at the expense of the democrats.

The ardent segregationists in the Oklahoma Democratic Party responded to this pressure. Lee Cruce, a banker from Ardmore who later challenged Haskell for the Democratic nomination for Governor, said that the Constitutional Convention delegates owed it to the people to put segregation into the document they were framing. Stafford, in a fiery editorial, asked:

> Since when did the president become our dictator? Where does he get his authority for telling us what to do and what not to do? And why should our constitutional convention seek to incorporate provisions which conform to his wishes rather than the wishes of the people who elected it?

Stafford buttressed his position by printing letters to the editor which supported the segregationist viewpoint. One letter writer to the *Oklahoman* compared the delegates to the Constitutional Convention to weak-kneed serfs who trembled at a rumour about what Roosevelt might do if they included segregation in their document. To obtain additional support for such views Stafford contacted William Jennings Bryan for his opinion. Bryan was the idol of mid-western American farmers because of his brilliant oratory on their behalf, and his repeated campaigns for the Presidency against candidates supported by big business interests. A deeply religious man, Bryan would later argue the prosecution's case against the teaching of evolution in the classroom during the famous Scopes "Monkey Trial" in Tennessee in the 1920s. At this point in his career Bryan was more concerned with political issues, and in a telegraphed answer to Stafford he urged the Constitutional Convention delegates to form their document to suit the people, and then let the Republicans take the blame for defeating it.

For their political kinsmen in the Twin Territories, Democrats in Washington tried to find out whether Roosevelt would in fact refuse to sign a statehood proclamation for Oklahoma because of segregation, but the President would not hint how he would act. This caused Republicans in the Territories to gloat that Teddy knew what the Democrats were up to and kept them guessing.

The affair soon took on a comic appearance. One anonymous wit penned a descriptive poem which became quite popular. Lampooning an African-American dialect the somewhat tortured verse went:

> Old Jim Crow! Old Jim Crow!
> Lawd a massy man we love you so.
> The Constitooshin's weak without you Jim.
> But dar's Teddy Roosevelt, we are scared of him.
> He squints, and he grins, but won't let us know.
> Just what to do with old Jim Crow.

While Stafford and the firm segregationists had considerable support the Haskell camp had a powerful ally in "Alfalfa Bill" Murray. As the President of the Constitution Convention, Murray had compelling power over the delegates, and because of his experience with the Sequoyah Constitution gathering he knew how to use it effectively.

Murray and Haskell decided to table the "Jim Crow" provision. Haskell first introduced a motion to the Convention to draft a segregation clause, and then to submit it to a panel of lawyers, chosen by the President of the convention, to review its legality. The motion passed, and Murray named to the committee delegates who had already announced their opposition to a segregation measure because it endangered statehood. Their opinion was a foregone conclusion, and the segregation provision died, at least for the time being.

Segregation may have been dead as a constitutional provision. Yet it was still an important issue within the Democratic Party. The question was debated by the Democrats following the Constitutional Convention, during their state primary election.*

During the Oklahoma Democratic primary the feud between Roy Stafford and Charles Haskell intensified. Stafford and his newspaper backed Lee Cruce, the Ardmore banker and a firm segregationist, as the Democratic nominee for Governor against Haskell.

. Stafford's Oklahoma City journal was a powerful factor within the Democratic party, but even it was no match for the organization and tactics of Haskell and his supporters. "Alfalfa Bill" did yeoman service among the farmers for his political ally. Murray even persuaded his brother to withdraw from the race for a state office when it appeared that his candidacy might harm Haskell.

Nor was the Haskell camp above using some questionable tactics. A Muskogee newspaper backing Haskell, perhaps because he owned it, accused one of Lee Cruce's organizers of being an ex-convict. From that point on in the campaign the Haskell forces referred to the Cruce supporters as the "damn Cruce convicts."

Haskell was able to take the Democratic Party nomination for Governor, but then faced the task of reuniting the party behind him, a process eased by the fact that hatred of African Americans was a convenient rallying point for the Democratic forces. No sooner had the date of the election for ratification of the State Constitution and the choosing of the first State officers been announced than the Democrats unmasked the racist strategy they were to use in the campaign.

On the day following the election announcement Roy Stafford sharpened his pencil and delivered an impassioned racist tirade in the pages of the *Oklahoman*. Stafford raised the ancient spectre of the "black rapist beast" in his attack upon the African-American supporters of the Republican party. Stafford even went so far as to condone lynching and other acts of violence against blacks because:

> The law is powerless to curb the debased, ignorant and brutal negro as it is to restrain vicious animals that attack man.

> Does not this alone explain the hangings, burnings and hor-

---

* A primary is an election within a political party to chose candidates for a general election.

rible forms of mob violence visited upon those of the black race who shatter the law?...

The doctrine of Christian Spirit and Mercy appeal to theoretical minds, but — practical north and south people will likely continue to use harsh methods to suppress the growing peril.

While not as passionate as Stafford the Democratic nominee for Governor also found African Americans to be convenient targets of election rhetoric. Haskell used the threat of an African-American migration to Oklahoma in his attacks on the Republicans' nominee for Governor, Frank Franz. According to Haskell the prospect of more African Americans moving to the new state was also the reason why segregation laws had to be brought in during the first sessions of the legislature.

In a keynote address in the town of South McAlester, Haskell said that he did not want to be extreme or radical on the race question. Rather, he wished to call attention to a serious situation. Nothing, he emphatically urged, would destroy the great prospects of the new state more than giving African Americans complete social equality. Haskell warned the white voters preparing to go to the polls that

If you by a majority vote, put your stamp of approval upon the men who are on the Republican state ticket and upon the state and local platforms...you thereby extend an open and cordial welcome to the negro race of other states, and it is not overestimating to say that Mississippi, Louisiana, Texas and Arkansas will practically become depopulated of the negro race by their grand rush to the new state....

These racist appeals were effective, and the Democrats dominated the first government of Oklahoma. The popular desire for statehood was reflected in the majority by which the Constitution was approved - 180,333 to 73,059. The Democrats' success was also reflected in the composition of the House and Senate of the new state. There were thirty-nine Democrats to five Republicans in the first State Senate, and ninety-three Democrats to just sixteen Republicans in the House. Charles N. Haskell won the Governor's chair by a count of 137,579 to 110,293 for the Republican nominee.

In the race for Governor a significant development, which had repercussions for African Americans, was the almost ten thousand votes cast for a Socialist Party candidate. The Socialist vote was important, because it was at the expense of the Democrats' vote, while at the same time the Republicans regrouped and rebounded. The growing threat to their political control of the state government would be the principal factor behind the Democrats' ultimately successful drive to take away African-Americans' right to vote in Oklahoma. That development, more than any other, was to send many more black Oklahomans to Canada in search of a new refuge.

"Alfalfa Bill" Murray was elected to the first Oklahoma House of Representatives, and then won the Speaker's chair. His first appointments symbolized the uniting of the North and the South in the new state, as well as the blacks' role. A Union and a Confederate veteran were each appointed to the honourary positions of House doorkeepers, and an African American was made the janitor. The Democrats moved quickly to legislate into existence what Murray's appointments had merely symbolized. In the House the very first bill introduced was a segregation measure, while in the Senate a similar piece of legislation was only the fourth bill introduced.

During the first legislative session, there was also discussion of revoking African Americans' right to vote. Nothing came of these early deliberations because many white Democrats believed that it was to their advantage to let African Americans continue to vote. Murray, for example, argued that in largely black areas white Republicans could finally be persuaded to vote for white Democrats in order to keep African Americans out of office. Such forecasts were overly optimistic, and in only three years the Democrats would take up the task of eliminating black votes from the state's ballot boxes.

While the Democrats' racial appeals helped them to gain political control of the new state they also created a climate of civil unrest. African Americans had long been targets for white violence, but the debate on segregation intensified white racial passions. Relegated to second-class citizenship, and depicted as beasts, African Americans were once more the victims of hate-crazed whites whose brutal actions were tolerated by society.

Nor was the racial violence long in coming. A race riot was narrowly averted in the town of Chickasaw when the Constitutional Convention was still in session. African-American workers had been brought into the area, and this had provoked a fight with local whites. In the town of Waurika a band of "white cappers" made an appearance, and gave the town's African-American population twenty-four hours to pack up and leave. The African-American residents of the burg summoned the sheriff of a nearby town who arrived with a heavily armed posse to try to bring calm to the situation.

In 1907 in the town of Holdenville a black man was viciously beaten for allegedly insulting a white woman. African Americans from the surrounding area banded together, and threatened to attack the town. Local whites were forced to post a heavy guard. Meanwhile, another band of "white cappers" appeared near Oklahoma City, threatening an African American farmer who had identified two whites as cattle thieves.

A particularly explosive situation developed at Henryetta, a town east of the black settlements of Boley and Clearview, and in an area which later produced several migrants to Canada. James Garden, a black man, was accused of slaying a white stable operator. On the day before Christmas, 1907, a mob of over one hundred whites marched to the jail, and extracted a confession. Garden was then hauled from the jail, hanged from a telegraph pole in the centre of town, and his body riddled with bullets.

African Americans from the town fled to Muskogee for fear of more violence. Several homes belonging to blacks were burnt, and their occupants driven out. Whites in the town then prepared for an attack as rumours circulated that African Americans from the surrounding district were planning to take revenge on the community. Every able-bodied white male was sworn in as a deputy. A band of heavily armed African Americans was reported to have passed through the nearby black settlement of Wildcat on its way to Henryetta, urging others to join them. Governor Haskell was made aware of the explosive situation, and ordered two companies of the state militia to be ready if more violence developed. The tension in the area gradually subsided, and the troops were not needed .

The militia was needed only a year later to quell a race riot in Okmulgee, just north of Henryetta. The violence began when an African American and an aboriginal got into a fight. The black man felled the other with a brick, and then sought refuge in a nearby house. He fought off attempts to dislodge him, killing four men and wounding eight others before he himself was badly wounded. The house he was defending was set on fire, forcing the black fugitive to flee, but he was captured and thrown back into the flames.

The vigilante handling of the black man started the riot. Three whites and four African Americans were killed before the troops sent by Governor Haskell arrived to restore order.

The Oklahoma segregation laws came into effect on 1 February 1908, and prompted more violence. African Americans fought back when their rights were restricted, and sometimes took out their frustration with violence of their own. When several African-American homes were dynamited at Cushing a black newspaper editor advised his readers to use their rifles and shot guns at close range with "nerve and pluck."

African Americans in Oklahoma let their feelings be known in a variety of ways. A group headed by the Lieutenant Governor of the new state was attacked by a black man protesting his segregation. In Muskogee local African Americans refused to obey the new laws until the county attorney ordered that they be vigorously enforced. When a train carrying prominent Democrats to a convention in Muskogee passed through the black town of Red Bird the residents attacked it with stones and chunks of coal. A single African-American male also stoned another train because he had been made to follow the new segregation laws.

These African-American protests against segregation had little if any effect. Racial segregation was bitter-tasting fruit, especially for African Americans who had already moved west to escape its effects. Since the days of slavery there had, nevertheless, been another way for blacks to escape white racism. Like peoples the world over, when African Americans could no longer tolerate the conditions they encountered, they left to find a better life elsewhere. Some looked to Africa for an escape route, while others preferred to stay and fight.

No sooner had the results of the first state election been announced than a wealthy African American from Okmulgee let it be known that he was going on a tour of various African kingdoms to find a place to colonize his fellow black Americans. He declared that blacks should be separated from whites, have a government of their own, and that it was his desire to lead a movement back to Africa. This appeal had a ready audience in Oklahoma, as did a petition campaign in the state during the summer of 1909 which asked for funds from the United States federal government for transportation to Liberia.

Not all African Americans in Oklahoma welcomed or supported these migration proposals. One black newspaper editor vented his feelings on the petition movement by declaring:

> We are not tired of fighting against unjust discrimination and we will never give up the fight until God says to us the victory is on the side of right lay you [sic] armour by. Right will win.

Still others began to look north to Canada. The implementation of racial segregation was a crucial factor in spurring groups of African Americans in Oklahoma to head for western Canada. They had been aware of Canada's desire for settlers for some time, but only a few had decided to investigate opportunities north of the forty-ninth parallel. When "Jim Crow" arrived on the stage, however, there was a noticeable increase in the number of African Americans heading toward the northern lights.

During the last decades of the nineteenth century and the first decades of the twentieth the federal government of Canada campaigned extensively in the American mid-west and Great Plains regions attempting to lure farmers to their "Last Best West." The Canadians became particularly interested in the Twin Territories, and later Oklahoma, because it was apparent that many more settlers were heading there than could be accommodated. Eventually the Canadian government sent an agent to the area to help promote its western agricultural lands.

The Canadian federal government also undertook an extensive advertising program in the area, combining glowing advertisements with economic inducements. These advertisements were found in African-American newspapers in Oklahoma, likely placed by contracted press services more concerned with readership numbers than with complexion. One Oklahoma black newspaper carried an item which described western Canada as being warmer than Texas. Other similar advertisements were carried by this same journal in subsequent years. None of the advertisements gave any indication that African Americans would be unwelcome.

While the implementation of racial segregation in Oklahoma sent some of the state's African-American residents toward Canada, it did not deter others from heading to the new state. The dreams of land, liberty, and the pursuit of happiness were as deeply ingrained in African-American minds as anyone else's. As bad as Oklahoma was becoming for the sons and daughters of Africa, it still appeared attractive for blacks living in the older southern states.

This continuing immigration was closely watched by those with political ambitions. Oklahoma's white Democrats had decided not to remove African-American voting rights during the first state legislature, but in just three years had changed their minds. By 1910 Oklahoma's Democrats were clamouring for disfranchisement as the Socialist Party cut deep into their strength, the Republicans rebounded from their previous defeats, and new African-American Republican voters streamed into the state.

It was obvious to everyone that the 1910 Oklahoma election would be a very close contest. It would be far too close for some white Democrats, and they set about ensuring their victory by limiting African-American voting rights. That development would spark a renewed African-American interest in western Canada, and propel white Canadians to take drastic action of their own to stop black immigration into the country.

Chapter Four

THE POLITICS OF RACISM

Four million southern negroes are looking towards Oklahoma. Continue our present system of negro suffrage and they will be our future neighbors. Adopt the grandfather amendment and the state will be saved from negro domination.

Shall Oklahoma be negroid or anglo-saxon?
— Editorial, Okemah, *Oklahoma Ledger,*
28 July 1910.

D isfranchising the African-American voter became an issue in Oklahoma because the Democratic Party there was severely jolted by the sudden resurgence of their political enemies, the Republicans. The Republicans had run ineffectual campaigns for the Constitutional Convention election in 1906, and for election of the first state officials in 1907. The Republicans altered their tactics, and began to question what they saw as the waste, inefficiency, and corruption of Charles Haskell's regime as governor.

In the election of 1908, Republican standing in both the State Senate and House increased. The Democrats were particularly stung by the election of an African-American legislator for the Republicans, Albert C. Hamlin. Even more disastrous was the loss of three federal House of Representatives seats to the Republicans. White Democrats realized that the solidly Republican African-American voter had played a key role in their setback. They quickly took up the task of eliminating the threat posed by such voters.

The Republican resurgence would not have been so serious for the Democrats, and they may not have bothered with the African-American voter, had it not been that the rise of the Socialist Party was reducing their own vote count. Oklahoma had a strong radical agrarian tradition, and supported a vigorous People's Party until the Populists fused with the Democrats in the late 1890s. The Socialists continued that tradition, although they were not merely a continuation of Populism.

The Oklahoma "Reds" were a diverse group. What separated them from their predecessors was their recruiting of landless rural workers into a movement which pointed to the landlord farmer as another form of capitalist villain. Oklahoma, especially the southern portion of the state, responded to their appeals.

Farm tenancy had grown dramatically since the first settlers arrived in the area bordering Texas, and had reached an astonishing fifty-four percent by 1910. In Marshall County, in southeast Oklahoma, it was eighty-one percent that year. Given the tenant farmer's poverty, and the "Reds" gospel of hope, it is not surprising that the Socialists increased their vote in the southern counties of Oklahoma in every election from 1907 to 1914.

In late 1909 the Socialists had launched a special "Farm Program," which appealed directly to the discontented farmers. The result was important Socialist gains across the southern counties of Oklahoma, and in 1910 the "Reds" tried to break the two-party system dominating the state's politics.

The southern counties were the Democrats' stronghold and, while they did not panic, some began to realize that their political hold on the state was loosening. Robert L. Williams, a future state governor, was one of the first to see the gravity of the situation. Williams was an Alabaman who had been a circuit preacher before settling in what was to become Oklahoma. He had turned to practising law, gradually emerged as a key figure in the Democratic Party, and became a judge after statehood. Williams recognized that the Socialists were successfully recruiting former Democrats and Populists, and that few of the "Reds" had ever been Republican supporters.

Williams also realized that their Constitutional Convention and state election victories had made his party overconfident. With success, factions had developed within the Democratic Party, and there was now considerable infighting. Still, Williams feared that

51

the Democrats' decline since 1907 was due less to these internal rivalries than it was to the rise of the Socialists.

Other Democrats recognized the Socialist challenge, but felt that they could deal with it. When A.A. Lesueur, a banker in southeastern Oklahoma, contacted Williams in May of 1910 he noted:

> I find that our population has increased in the County one hundred per cent since 1907. Very little of this increase is negro. While we have something of an increase in the Socialist vote, we have fair reasons to believe this more than offset by the fact that our growth is largely from Arkansas and Texas and unpoisoned by this new virus.

Williams was likely better able to appreciate his party's predicament because of the perspective he derived from his contacts across the state. He regularly received indications of the electorate's mood from friends and supporters. One such contact wrote to Williams to point out that the Democrats had to watch the Republicans closely at that point, adding that the party workers could not afford to trifle or lie down on their jobs. A fellow jurist, Judge F.L. McCain of Muskogee, was even more emphatic regarding the situation when he wrote to Williams early in 1910:

> It is with deepest regret that I have to say that, unless there is a radical change in public sentiment, the democrats can not hope to carry this state next fall. If it were possible for the legislature to pass an election law with [an] emergency clause by which we could get rid of a large portion of the negro vote, there might be some hope but under the present system of voting it is out of the question. The negro will mark under the eagle no matter who is put up for candidates. This I know for a moral certainty...

McCain concluded by arguing that he did not believe "Jesus Christ could carry the democratic ticket at the next election."

Judge McCain's suggestion to disfranchise the African-American voters of the state was not new, but the rise of the Socialists and the resurgence of the Republicans gave it a practical urgency. The southern counties were the Democrats' stronghold, a stronghold being weakened by the Socialist attack. Any decline in the Democrats' voting strength lessened their chances of holding off the charging Republicans.

Leading Democrats such as Judges Williams and McCain felt that unless something drastic was done before the 1910 election they might find themselves in opposition to a Republican governor, or even a Republican legislature. For southern white Democrats this heralded a return to the "carpetbaggism" and "black domination" of the Reconstruction era following the Civil War, and in stopping it anything was permissible. It was in this climate that the Democratic Party of Oklahoma forsook its name and moved to institute Mississippi's infamous "Grandfather Clause."

The Grandfather Clause was an amendment to the state constitution which required eligible voters to be able to read and write, but exempted them if they or one of their ancestors had voted before 1861. Illiterate whites were allowed to vote if they showed that their grandfathers had used their franchise before the slaves had been freed. African-American voters, with a supposedly high illiteracy rate, did not qualify for the exemption and were therefore penalized for the colour of their skin.

Still, Oklahoma's African-American population had an illiteracy rate of less than twenty percent in 1910, thanks to the Indian and Territorial schools. This was substantially better than the national average for African Americans at the time. Yet with the "Grandfather" measure, a black Oklahoman even if literate, could still lose the vote. How the legislation was enforced was a key factor. It was quite simple for the Democrat-appointed election officials of the state's notoriously partisan Election Board to find all African-American voters illiterate.

There is tragic irony in the manner in which the Oklahoma Democrats went about disfranchising the state's African-American voters. The Democrats were imbued with the spirit of frontier democracy, and believed fervently that the people should have a direct voice in their political affairs. To insure the people's input the Oklahoma State Constitution included the then radically innovative measures known as the Initiative and Referendum provisions. These clauses allowed the electors of the state to initiate legislation if a certain number of them petitioned for it, and for a state-wide referendum to be held to validate any such proposal. It was these measures, designed to increase democracy, which the Democrats used to decrease it by removing African-American voting rights.

To ensure a victory for a Grandfather Clause amendment to the state's Constitution the Democrats manipulated the election laws governing the Initiative and Referendum provisions. During a special session of the legislature State Senator Taylor, a Democrat, proposed a number of changes to these laws, including allowing the legislature as well as the people of the state to initiate a proposal. Taylor also suggested an altered ballot, which was designed to confuse and mislead the electorate, and procedures obviously intended to count as many votes for a "Grandfather Clause" proposal as was possible.

Not all Democrats supported or endorsed the course of action proposed by Taylor. The United States Senator from Oklahoma, Thomas P. Gore, argued that

> It seems to me that it would be well for the Legislature to recall or revise the Taylor election law. I doubt if it would be ratified at the polls. It is a complicated piece of machinery, and the average voter votes against what he does not understand.

Gore recognized the need for some kind of franchise manipulation to deal with his party's fear of black voters, but he apparently wanted it dealt with in the legislature and not in an election. Gore may have had in mind a voter registration law such as the Democrats did implement in 1916. In any case he was prepared to risk some Democratic losses, noting to his friend Judge Williams that the only real peril was a Republican Governor, House, and Senate at the same time, and that was very unlikely.

Senator Gore was clearly concerned that the Democrats were risking defeat by going to the electorate with the proposed Grandfather Clause. Judge Williams was sympathetic to this opinion, and later in the year wrote to Gore that, "To my mind, if this amendment is defeated when it is submitted to the voters of the state, it will imperil the Democratic ticket, because it would destroy the confidence of the Democratic voter of their ability to succeed". Gore had by now changed his mind on the issue, recognizing that Taylor's methods of manipulating the vote count would ensure a victory. He then wrote to Williams, "I am glad that the Grandfather Clause has been submitted and under the method of voting it will undoubtedly prevail. It ought to prevail under any method of voting".

The correspondence between Williams and Gore illustrates the concern leading Democrats had for their party's course of

"Black Indians" obtaining aboriginal land grants, Fort Gibson, Oklahoma

E. P. McCabe

African-American settlers in the Creek Nation, near Pecan Mission, Oklahoma

Archives and Manuscripts Division of the Oklahoma Historical Society

"Alfalfa Bill" Murray

C. N. Haskell

R. L. Williams

A.C. *Hamlin*

action. That very concern also underlines their recognition of the gravity of their situation. Unless something drastic was done, and done quickly, their hold on the state government would be challenged by the Republicans and the Socialists. Loyal Democrats thought that their scheme would solve this problem, but then encountered opposition from an unexpected source.

Governor Charles Haskell, when presented with Senator Taylor's bill for his signature, objected to several of its features and vetoed it. Haskell was worried about possible legal repercussions, specifically that the bill might be declared unconstitutional. The Governor pointed to a number of potential problems, although he did not object to the intent of the legislation, for he ultimately signed a virtually identical bill.

Haskell perhaps recognized that long court battles over election returns were a distinct possibility. The bill was too loose for someone of Haskell's apparent precise legal instincts, and he seems to have felt that it would be better to pass a more sound bill rather than to have to do it later. As one Republican critic of the Taylor measure indicated it was difficult to determine if Haskell used his veto, "because the bill was too rotten or not rotten enough."

The Grandfather Clause campaign was not the "Jim Crow" segregation debate. In this battle the Democrats were fighting for their political lives. This time they were not about to tolerate Haskell's fears and, as one disgruntled State Senator declared, the Senate would remain in session as long as it took to pass an election law. The disfranchisers responded quickly and on 8 March 1910, the day after these remarks were made, introduced a new version of the bill. Faced with this intransigence Governor Haskell signed the new bill into law on 17 March 1910.

The date the legislation became law was important because the Democrats needed time to collect the approximately thirty-eight thousand signatures needed on their Initiative petition. They wanted the State Constitution altered before the 1910 election in November, and the only pollings before that time were the state primaries in early August. Unless the signatures on the petition were gathered quickly there might not be enough time to arrange for a Grandfather Clause to be voted on by the electorate in the summer.

To help their campaign the Democrats used the tactic that had worked so well in Haskell's race for Governor, and on the segregation issue. They whipped up white fear of a massive black immigration into the state. The tactic was simple, and effective. As one Democratic editor stated, when he asked his readers if they had signed the petition,

> Oklahoma is the one Southern State where negroes vote and hold office. Unless you are willing for this state to continue to be the dumping ground for the negroes of the whole south, sign the petition and help preserve Oklahoma and her state government to the white race while there is yet time.

Despite their doubts about going to the electorate with the Grandfather Clause, loyal Democrats such as Judge Williams and Senator Gore responded to the signature campaign. Williams used his extensive network of contacts across the state to help obtain signatures. For example, on 15 May 1910 Williams, in a postscript on a letter regarding a legal case, urged the acquisition of at least a thousand signatures in his correspondent's area, and suggested that loyal Democrats in nearby towns be notified to get moving collecting more signatures.

Writing from Washington, Senator Gore had a suggestion for Williams. He mentioned a letter from a supporter in Oklahoma who had said the amendment should carry there because the people were tired of "ourang-outang government." While admitting that it was a cruel thing to say the Senator apparently missed the irony of the remark — the Democrats were the government in Oklahoma — and suggested that "'down with ourang-outang government' quietly circulated would make a good slogan."

African Americans living in Oklahoma recognized the seriousness of the Democrats' campaign, and reacted strongly against it. As one black editor phrased it, the proposed amendment to the state constitution was, "the paramount issue with the Negro of the state of Oklahoma," while another urged all African Americans in the state to fight it. African Americans poured torrents of abuse on the Democrats' proposed amendment. It was "one of the most vicious pieces of legislation ever enacted in any state," "Rot of the most damnable nature," and "an unpardonable sin." One African-American group characterized the proposed voting change as "a child of Hades and in league with the devil... a measure advocated by a set of men in furtherance of selfish ends...."

African Americans discovered that on this issue, recognizing their party's existence was being threatened, white Republicans were their allies. The Chairman of the Republican State Committee fought to have the "liberty stealing laws" referred to a fair vote, realizing that without such a move his party might die in Oklahoma. One Republican newspaper editor argued that the Democrats' proposal was against the spirit of the United States Constitution, and later charged that:

> The proposed grandfather clause amendment to the constitution is unfair and unconstitutional because it aims to disfranchise one class of illiterates and not all classes. The spirit of our laws is to treat all persons with equal and exact justice. Oklahoma should be the last state to think of swerving from that high ideal.

The Democrats pressed ahead with their signature campaign. By the end of May, 1910, they had collected over forty thousand signatures on their Initiative. The Democrats claimed that it had taken them just over one month to get the required number. This was a record, it was said, and clear evidence that the voters supported their attempt to eliminate the ignorant from voting.

In the flush of the petition campaign's success Oklahoma's Democrats argued that amending the state's constitution to limit African-American voting was the most satisfactory and the most logical solution to the state's racial and African-American immigration problems. If the Grandfather Clause was adopted, it was claimed, the massive African-American migration heading toward Oklahoma would turn elsewhere. If the constitution was not revised, then it was predicted that in less than five years half of the counties in the state would be ruled by African Americans. This would have fulfilled E.P. McCabe's dream. For white Democrats, however, it was a nightmare.

While amending the state constitution to stop African-American voting was designed by the Democrats to weaken the Republican vote it was the leadership of the Socialist Party which campaigned most effectively against it. The Socialists focused their attack upon Taylor's State Senate bill which had allowed the Democrats to initiate the measure. In an undated argument submitted to Oklahoma's Secretary of State, which attempted to derail the Democrats' campaign, the Socialists argued that the Senate bill was "the most infamous piece of legislation passed by the reactionaries now in power." According to the "Reds" the legislation perverted the intent of the Initiative and Referendum clause of the state constitution, and when the Democrats passed it they

> plunged a knife into the bowels of the Initiative and Referendum and turned it around. There is nothing left of the Initiative and Referendum in this State but a new made grave. If there are those who weep and wish to erect a monument over the remains I suggest this as an epitaph — "Assassinated by Legislative Chicanery and Executive debauchery with Judicial sanction."

The Socialists also turned their printing presses against the Grandfather Clause. Their noted agitator, Oscar Ameringer, wrote a twenty-five thousand word statement against the measure, and it was circulated throughout Oklahoma. The idea was to take advantage of a clause in the state constitution which allowed arguments of such length to be made on each side of an Initiative. While ultimately unsuccessful, the Socialists took justifiable pride in their efforts. There is evidence that they were able to swing proportionately more votes against "Grandfather" than the Republicans.

The Socialists' campaign might have been even more successful had it not been disrupted by a racist strain which appeared in their ranks. The official party policy was against the Democrats' measure, and prominent leaders spoke against it. Still, "Red" newspapers in the pivotal southern counties of Oklahoma openly stated that African Americans could never expect to have full equality with whites.

As hard as they tried, the combined efforts of African Americans, Republicans, and the Socialists could not match the Democrats' tactics and campaign. On 2 August 1910 Oklahomans decided the African-American voters' fate when they approved the Grandfather Clause amendment to their state's constitution. The final vote was 134,443 in favour with 106,222 opposed.

While it is difficult to determine how many African Americans lost their voting rights a reasonable estimate would be approximately twenty-one thousand, although one source suggested that it was closer to thirty thousand voters. The Democrats rejoiced at their success, and gloated over how well "Grandpa" ran for such an old man. African Americans living in Oklahoma continued to fight the decision of their white neighbours, yet hundreds of them appear to have recognized the futility of such efforts, and instead began to make plans to leave the state.

These African-American emigrants were also propelled by the fact that the Democrats, leaving nothing to chance to ensure victory in the upcoming Fall campaign, continued their racist attacks. African Americans might no longer have had the vote in Oklahoma, but that did not diminish their value as scapegoats. African Americans were also a necessary target for the Democrats because their primary to choose candidates, which paralleled the Grandfather Clause endorsement campaign, revealed deep divisions within their ranks. By focusing upon their hatred of African Americans the Democrats provided a necessary rallying point for supporters otherwise badly divided over who would be the new candidate for Governor.

When African Americans tried to make their way to the polls, in November of 1910, they discovered they had to deal with more than partisan racial assaults. Even though the Grandfather Clause amendment was aimed at illiterates, black Oklahomans who could read and write found that they were not allowed to vote. How the amendment was applied was crucial, and before the election Governor Haskell had made it abundantly clear that in order to vote an African American would have to be able to read like a professor.

Even college level abilities were not enough for some election inspectors when polling began, and one African American who could read and write not only English but Greek and Latin as well was turned away from the voting booth. African-American professional men presented themselves at one polling station armed with affidavits testifying to their voting competency, but were turned down. Several of them began reading sections of the State Constitution aloud, only to again be denied. Some finally voted after trying three or four times. Literate African-American voters were turned away at other stations for trivial reasons.

Even when an African-American voter overcame these obstacles there was no guarantee that the ballot was counted. A deputy sheriff in one town caught a Democratic election judge stuffing African-American ballots into his boots instead of into the ballot box. When challenged, the Democrat said he would not allow a "nigger lover" to boss him, and struck the deputy. The law man knocked him down, and presumably took him to jail. What became of the ballots is a mystery.

As serious as the denial of their democratic rights was for African Americans, occasionally one of them would use humour to make a point. A brief rain storm disrupted balloting in one town, and at the height of the squall an African American entered the polling station. He began to read aloud from some materials at hand while the Democrat election inspectors smugly waited to refuse him the right to vote. They were surprised, however, that he stopped reading and turned to head out the door when the rain stopped. When asked if he was planning to try to vote the African American said no, he wasn't, he had just stepped in to get out of the rain.

It was indeed a rainy day for democracy as the legislative juggling, the Grandfather Clause, the racial appeals, and the election manipulation had their intended effect, and the Democrats retained their hold on power in Oklahoma. Still, the result was very close, and the final returns show that the Democrats had good reason to be concerned with their political situation. Lee Cruce, attempting to succeed his rival Haskell as Governor, polled 120,218 votes for the Democrats, the Republican nominee McNeal garnered 99,527, while J.T. Cumbie, the Socialist candidate for Governor, more than doubled his party's 1907 count by taking 24,707 votes.

An analysis of these returns shows how important eliminating African-American votes was to the Democrats' success. If half of the approximately twenty-one thousand disfranchised black voters had cast ballots for McNeal, then he would have been within eleven thousand votes of toppling Cruce. If three-quarters of the missing African American votes had gone to McNeal, he would have been within two thousand votes of Cruce. If all of the missing black ballots had gone to the Republican, a not unrealistic possibility, McNeal would have been Governor.

African Americans who had moved to Oklahoma to find land and liberty now found that they had come full circle. They had escaped second-class citizenship and racial discrimination only to be engulfed once more. They fought this new situation as they always had by organizing and going to court, resisting physically when they could, and leaving when they felt there was no other choice. Early in 1911 there were rumours of a pending black migration to New Mexico, but this was frowned upon by those who preferred to stay and fight. Others had had enough of Oklahoma and were determined to leave, thereby serving notice that they would not accept second-class citizenship. But New Mexico was not their destination, nor any part of the United States. These African Americans looked north toward Canada.

Canada's thirst for settlers had not slackened since Oklahoma had achieved statehood, and advertisements promoting land in western Canada continued to appear in Oklahoma newspapers. Democratic, Republican, black, and white journals all sang the glowing qualities of Canada's West. Wheat yields of from twenty-five to thirty-five bushels per acre were possible, it was said, and no finer wheat could be found anywhere.

Oklahomans were told that their countrymen were streaming into Canada. In a direct appeal to the landless tenants of the state, the Canadians asked why the Oklahomans would continue to rent a farm when there was free land available to the north. If these renters had the mistaken impression that Canada was nothing more than a snowy wasteland, then these Canadian advertisements also went to considerable lengths to overcome that negative image.

The Canadian federal government was not the only organization advertising western Canadian land in Oklahoma. The Canadian Pacific Railroad maintained an office in Oklahoma City, handing out brochures and arranging charters to discover "Sunny Alberta." Together these agencies made it a simple task for any Oklahoman, black or white, to find out how to get to Canada and obtain land there.

The Canadian campaign attracted small numbers of African Americans even before racial segregation arrived in Oklahoma. Seymour and James Lowery filed homestead applications for Canadian land on 15 August 1904. They apparently convinced another family member, Jesse, to accompany them because he filed on 25 November 1904. The three men, together with Jesse's wife and child, left what would become Oklahoma and took up residence in March, 1905, near Maidstone in what would soon become the Canadian province of Saskatchewan. Richard (Dick) Lawson followed the same route when he brought his wife and two children to the area in November, 1906, having filed his application the previous year.

African Americans living in other states were also attracted by the opportunity to obtain Canadian land. Three brothers named Lafayette moved north from Iowa during this period. They settled near Rosetown in west central Saskatchewan where a number of their descendants still live.

The states and provinces of the Great Plains

Canada was advertising its western lands in African American territorial and state newspapers from at least 1905, but these had attracted only a few black settlers. When racial segregation was implemented in 1908, and racial violence increased, there was a spurt of migration activity. Western Canada became an attractive alternative for African Americans who had come west - it offered land, and apparently freedom from prejudice.

Tony Payne, one of the first black settlers in Wildwood, Alberta, moved from Canadian County, Oklahoma, to the real Canada in 1908. Twenty African-American families from the state soon followed. Anderson N. Harper, formerly of Indiana, moved his family from Oklahoma to the Maidstone area of Saskatchewan in May of 1908. Peter Taler had been born in Georgia, and had moved to Oklahoma. He moved his wife and child to Canada very quickly, filing his homestead application in August, 1908, and taking up residence in October of that year. Cecil J. Lane had been born in Virginia, but had moved to Oklahoma. He and his wife Emma moved with their ten children from Tabor, Oklahoma, to Maidstone, Saskatchewan, in September, 1910, after filing an application in October of 1909.

Segregation was certainly a major factor in Jeff Edwards' decision to leave Oklahoma for the Amber Valley area of Alberta. He had first become interested in western Canada, he claimed, when Oklahoma began its segregation policies. The African Americans who went north to eastern Canada were fleeing slavery, he would claim, while those on the Canadian Plains had fled something just as bad - racial segregation.

Jeff Edwards did not leave for Canada until 1910. He had become interested in a trek north, but that interest had to be renewed by the departure of his future father-in-law, Jordan Murphy, and his two sons. One of the sons was Edwards' best friend, and he decided to join them.

On the train to Canada Edwards met another African American, Henry Sneed, who was also headed north. The party had no trouble crossing the international boundary and, after stopping in Winnipeg, Manitoba, for awhile, they headed north-west toward Alberta. Sneed later returned to Oklahoma to organize a larger party of African-American emigrants. He was to have trouble getting this larger party into Canada though because white Canadians had become concerned with a possible black influx, and were taking steps to stop it.

African Americans living in Oklahoma, who were attracted by government and railroad advertising, found other reasons to become interested in moving to Canada. Shortly after the Grandfather Clause amendment was introduced in the state legislature, a white newspaper editor penned a lengthy commentary on how pleased farmers returning from trips to Canada were with the law enforcement in the northern dominion. This journalist found it odd that in the United States, where everyone said they were in favor of vigorous law enforcement, so many laws were laxly enforced and in some cases were even farcical. Was it any wonder there were lynchings in Oklahoma, he pondered, noting that there were never such crimes under the British flag because of effective law enforcement. This journalist concluded that while people were always talking about the crimes of African Americans, such incidents were hardly surprising when whites themselves scoffed at and disregarded the law.

Only a short time later this particular newspaper editor produced another lengthy story on Canadian law enforcement. This article focused upon the Mounted Police, and noted how they had firmly established British law in western Canada. The Oklahoma journalist also noted:

> There has never been a lynching in Canada. Put that down to the credit of the mounted police, who administered justice so successfully that there was never any temptation for the work to be taken up by private enterprise.

The image of Canada as a safe, law-abiding country, with plenty of free land for settlers, appealed to many Oklahomans. African Americans living in the state had particular reasons to turn north. When these black freedom seekers did decide to move once again they did it quickly, and in such numbers that it attracted attention on both sides of the forty-ninth parallel.

African-American Oklahomans intent on migrating to Canada waited until the Spring of 1911 to leave, giving themselves enough time to sell their property and to settle their affairs. In March of that year there was a report of ninety black families, totalling some five hundred people, leaving Okfuskee County in east central Oklahoma for Canada. The colonization movement was also strong in Muskogee and Creek Counties. It was claimed that one thousand African-American families, or seven thousand people, were preparing to leave, but the total migration never did reach such proportions. Still, the reasons for leaving were well-known: According to one source, "They are leaving Oklahoma because of adverse legislation, 'Jim Crow' work and depot laws, the 'grandfather clause' act that prohibits them from voting, separate school laws and others."

The African Americans who moved north confirmed the reports that they were fleeing segregation and disfranchisement. Arriving in St. Paul, Minnesota, in March of 1911, en route to western Canada, one group said that they had left Oklahoma because they were not allowed to vote. They also claimed that there were five thousand more African Americans waiting to follow them.

The spokesman for another group, which entered Canada in British Columbia, stated that, "The people of Oklahoma treat us like dogs. We are not allowed to vote and are not admitted to any of the theatres or public places. They won't even let us ride the streetcars in some of the towns." When asked what had attracted them to Canada he replied, "We heard about the free lands here and also that everyone had the right to vote and was a free man."

Segregation and disfranchisement sent between one thousand and fifteen hundred African-American Oklahomans northward. They refused to accept a return to the second-class citizenship they had come to Oklahoma to escape. They would soon discover that white Canadians were also infected with the racist virus, and were also prepared to use whatever means were available to them to stop African Americans from becoming their neighbours.

Chapter Five

RACISM ON THE NORTHERN PLAINS

The task of assimilating all the white people who enter our borders is quite a heavy enough one without the color proposition being added.
— Edmonton, *Capital*
16 April 1910.

The African Americans who left Oklahoma for western Canada were one element in a huge American migration to the region. Upwards of three quarters of a million Americans moved north to the plains of Canada in the last decade of the nineteenth century, and first decades of the twentieth. They discovered an area which was at once familiar, and strangely different.

Canada had been formed in 1867 by the union of four of the colonies in North America remaining British after the American Revolution. The joining of Canada East and Canada West (Quebec and Ontario), Nova Scotia, and New Brunswick was a defensive maneuver designed to thwart possible American annexation. The American Civil War had ended in 1865, and several bellicose American politicians had championed a foreign war as the best way to reunite their country. Their targets were the British colonies to the north. It was argued that taking them over would be one quick way to settle American war claims against Britain. Several raids into Canada by the Irish-American Fenian Brotherhood gave the challenge a degree of validity in the eyes of the Canadians.

The unification of the four former colonies in 1867 also gave the new entity of Canada increased borrowing and taxing powers. These were important tools for the ambitious bankers, merchants, and manufacturers of central Canada who influenced the new federal government, and who envisioned great business opportunities in the west. In 1869 Canada purchased the Hudson's Bay Company title to Rupert's Land, including the mid-west plains, and in 1871 persuaded the west coast colony of British Columbia to join the Dominion. A mounted police force was formed to keep the peace on the plains, and a transcontinental railroad was chartered to bind the new country together. A territorial government was established over much of the plains, and policies were developed which were designed to people the area with prosperous farmers.

American farmers found these land policies as familiar as the grasslands they claimed in Canada. Canadians may not have wanted to become part of the United States, but this did not stop shrewd Canadian politicians from borrowing from the American experience. Canada took the land-holding, marketing, and surveying systems of the United States and adapted them to its own Great Plains region.

There were, however, important differences, and it was these which American farmers moving north must have found strange. There was always a great deal more central government control over western Canada since the territorial government was directed from the nation's capital, Ottawa. Control was exercised through British parliamentary institutions, and not republican ones such as the Americans knew. There was also an effective means of enforcing government edicts — the increasingly famous red-coated Mounted Police.

Americans entering western Canada also discovered that unlike other areas of the continent which they had settled they would be sharing this region with other English-speaking people. Anglo-Canadians, particularly from Ontario, had been attracted by opportunities in the west. A large number of British immigrants had also found their way to the area. The Americans, British, and Anglo-Canadians shared a great deal — a language, a deep love of democracy, and a profound racist bias against dark-skinned peoples. Together, the three English-speaking groups dominated the infant society, and other immigrant groups conformed to their views.

While the settling of western Canada attracted people from across the United States, the upper mid-west produced the largest number of immigrants. This region had vigorously supported the anti-slavery movement, but had done so in an effort to keep African Americans from being brought west. The mid-west had also been

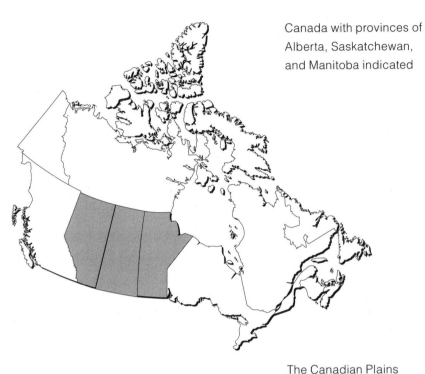

Canada with provinces of Alberta, Saskatchewan, and Manitoba indicated

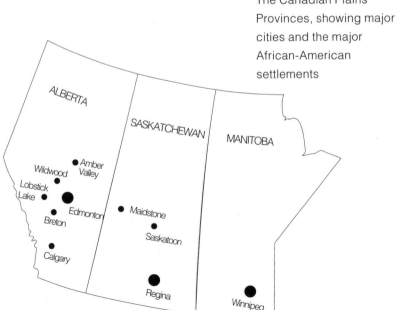

The Canadian Plains Provinces, showing major cities and the major African-American settlements

the birthplace of racial segregation before such practices moved south following the Civil War. Such racial attitudes moved with the region's sons and daughters to their new northern homes, and became entrenched there. One Saskatchewan pioneer, who had moved north as a child, vividly recalled that his father had said the reason they left Iowa was to "get away from the cyclones and the niggers."

British immigrants to the plains region of Canada also brought their racial attitudes with them. While Britain had abolished slavery in 1834 the worldwide expansion of its empire, made possible by technological superiority, served to confirm British views of their racial supremacy. For example, when a band of Jamaican peasants rioted in 1865 the much respected London *Times* had argued that,

> It seems impossible to eradicate the original savageness of the African blood. As long as the black man has a strong white Government and numerous white population to control him he is capable of living as a respectable member of society... But wherever he attains to a certain degree of independence there is the fear that he will resume the barbarous life and the fierce habits of his African ancestors...

Such attitudes were common in Victorian Britain, and were brought to western Canada by British immigrants. These prejudices easily fused with similar opinions held by Anglo-Canadians who had moved west. Objections to people of African ancestry settling on the plains were being raised in the East even before western Canadians voiced their disapproval of the idea. As early as 1899 the Immigration Branch of the Canadian federal Department of the Interior was replying negatively to the suggestion that African Americans be allowed to settle Canada's plains. The branch informed its agent in Kansas City that "it is not desired that any negro immigrants should arrive in Western Canada... or that such immigration should be promoted by our agents." When an African American from Shawnee, Oklahoma Territory, contacted Canadian authorities in 1902 on behalf of a group of prospective black settlers he was informed by L.M. Fortier, Secretary of the Department of the Interior, that "the Canadian Government is not particularly desirous of encouraging the immigration of negroes."

While eastern-based government officials may have wanted to stop more blacks from settling in the west they could not keep the plains white. There were already a few dark spots. People of African ancestry had very early found their way to western Canada and, while there were not many until after the turn of the century, they were among the region's true pioneers. The black fur trader, Henry Mills, worked at several fur trading posts on Canada's plains before that activity gave way to agriculture. His son David often served as an interpreter with the aboriginal nations. Colonel James Macleod of the Mounted Police employed a black nanny for his children while he oversaw the policing of the region. Perhaps the most famous African American to settle in western Canada was John Ware, a former slave who found his way north trailing the American cattle herds which stocked the region's early ranches, and who stayed to found one of his own south of present-day Calgary.

These few dark complexions did not raise white passions although the individuals likely encountered expressions of prejudice. John Ware, for example, was generally known as "Nigger John," and reputedly avoided going to Calgary because of the prejudice he encountered there. Instead, it was the aboriginal peoples of the region who felt the first sting of white racial attitudes.

Herded onto reserves once the bison on which they depended were driven to the edge of extinction, the aboriginals were supposed to be taught agriculture and helped to adapt to the new society. Instead they were subjected to racially based policies. These policies were designed to end their societies, and rob them of what little land they continued to hold.

Periodically someone would rebel at such treatment. Such was the case in 1895 when Almighty Voice, a young Cree in what would become the province of Saskatchewan, was arrested for cattle theft, escaped from jail, and killed a Mounted Police officer sent to arrest him. The fugitive was at large for over a year and, when cornered with two accomplices, killed three more men, two of them Mounties, and wounded two other policemen. The authorities obviously wanted no more of an American-style shoot-out. With calm Canadian efficiency they ordered two cannons to the locale, and had the fugitives shelled to death.

This incident aroused white racial passions across the northern plains, and these emotions found voice in the region's press. An Edmonton newspaper published an editorial in which Almighty Voice's supposed life was contrasted with his spectacular death. That life, according to this respected journal, was probably:

the usual humdrum existence of his brother redmen name-
ly, in turning up religiously on ration day to receive his stint
of government grub and endeavoring to steal as much [or]
more as he could lay his hands on. Occasionally, no doubt,
a break would come in the monotony of life, when a bottle
of forty-rod firewater surreptitiously introduced into the camp
would create a passing diversion and impart to the imbibing
redskin a momentary and entirely misleading impression
that he was predestined to do great deeds.

This journalist concluded that Almighty Voice's spirit must
now be full of pride at the excitement he had caused and "if he
has brains enough to reason with he could arrive at the very sen-
sible conclusion that by dying he became much more useful than
he ever could have been while living."

Such scathing racism was not uncommon in western Canada
then or in subsequent years, but it was rarely so virulent. The likely author of this diatribe was Frank Oliver, publisher and editor
of the Edmonton *Bulletin*.

Oliver had been born in 1853 in Peel County, in what is now the
province of Ontario. He came to the Canadian Plains as a young
man, and quickly established himself in public life. He served on
both the North-West Territorial Council, and in its successor the
Territorial Legislative Assembly.

Like Roy Stafford, his journalistic colleague in Oklahoma,
Oliver was a racist, and like the Oklahoman he was able to bring
his views to bear on public policy, although in a more personal
and direct fashion. At the moment that he published the outburst
on aboriginals, Frank Oliver was on the verge of a meteoric political career which would see him elected to the Canadian federal
Parliament for the Liberal party. He then became the federal
Minister of the Interior, responsible for both aboriginal affairs
and immigration at the time the African Americans began arriving from Oklahoma.

Frank Oliver and his fellow white western Canadians already
had pronounced views on dark-skinned peoples when the African
Americans began stepping down from the immigrant railroad cars.
Their prejudices were also being confirmed, and transmitted
throughout the developing society by the racist portrayal of blacks
in the region's newspapers. People of African ancestry were regularly the butt of jokes and cartoons in western journals. They

were also negatively portrayed in numerous advertisements. Minstrel shows, very popular at the time, frequently portrayed blacks as dupes and buffoons.

Far more serious were the sensationalist reports of exceptional contemporary stories involving African Americans. For example, in the spring of 1910 an Edmonton newspaper gave prominent coverage to the murder confession of a local African-American man. James Chapman had gone to the Mounted Police and admitted to having helped a white woman poison her husband in Stillwater, Oklahoma, over a year earlier. Chapman and the woman had then fled to Alberta.

While there was no connection between this story and the arrival of African-American immigrants at the time, it is significant that this news item appeared in the same issue of the newspaper as an item announcing the Edmonton Board of Trade's decision to try to stop the black trek. Given its portrayal of the two events it is also not surprising that less than a week later this same Edmonton newspaper would editorialize that:

> The Board of Trade has done well to call attention to the amount of negro immigration which is taking place into this district. It has already attained such proportions as to discourage white settlers from going into certain districts. The immigration department has no excuse for encouraging it at all...we prefer to have the southern race problem left behind. The task of assimilating all the white people who enter our borders is quite a heavy enough one without the colour proposition being added.

By the spring of 1910 there were already enough African-American settlers arriving in the district for the Edmonton Board of Trade to feel it was time for action on the issue. At its monthly meeting on 12 April, the board unanimously passed a resolution calling the federal government's attention to the "marked increase" in the black immigration to western Canada. The board said that it felt that the foundations for a "negro problem" were being laid. In the board's opinion the African Americans were a "most undesirable element," and it urged the authorities to take immediate action to stop more from entering the country.

Canadian immigration authorities were, in fact, already concerned with the developing black influx, and were trying to stop it. At first they tried to prevent immigration literature from reach-

ing African Americans in Oklahoma. When this proved haphazard immigration officials tried using vigorous medical examinations at the border as a deterrent. This latter maneuver proved to
be without value when healthy African-American men, women,
and children presented themselves for admission.

Henry Sneed was an African American from Texas who had
moved to Oklahoma. In 1910 he visited western Canada and apparently liked what he saw. In August of the same year he returned
to Clearview, Oklahoma, to begin organizing a large party of
African American emigrants. He had no trouble attracting
prospects due to Oklahoma's racial policies. Meetings were held
in Oklahoma, and in other states in the area, and early in 1911
emigrants from Oklahoma, as well as Kansas and Texas, gathered
in Weleetka, Oklahoma, to begin their trek.

Sneed's first large group of settlers consisted of 194 men,
women, and children. They were well prepared, having no less
than nine railroad carloads of horses and farm implements.
Another group of 200 people began gathering in the same town
soon after the first band departed, but before setting out waited
to hear if the first party would be allowed to enter Canada.

The African Americans had good reason to be cautious. In late
March 1911 the Sneed party was stopped at Emerson, Manitoba,
near the international boundary with Minnesota, while a rigorous medical examination was carried out. Their health, plus their
numbers, attracted considerable publicity. This publicity in turn
provoked comment, and revealed the deep racist feelings which
had taken root on the plains of Canada. Fearing that a further
attempt would be made to exclude them from Canada the leaders of the group appealed to Washington, D.C., and the United
States Consul in Ottawa was instructed to find out whether African
Americans, as a group, could be excluded under Canadian law. It
was determined that no such Canadian regulation then existed,
so the group was allowed to enter.

Still, prospective African-American migrants had to have been
uneasy with the situation. This was especially the case when an
Oklahoma newspaper reprinted a Kansas City journal's report
that "The exodus has been bitterly opposed by a large per cent of
the white population of the Canadian provinces." That they were
not wanted in western Canada would become increasingly clear
to the African Americans in the months ahead as Canada served
notice that it intended to keep the northern plains white.

When their Great Northern train arrived in Emerson, Manitoba, the Sneed group immediately attracted attention. The local newspaper reported the arrival of "men, women, and piccaninnies," and then commented that the town had been decorated with "coons" ever since. They had money, farm implements, and livestock, it continued, and were generally of a "good appearance." Still, African Americans were not the most desirable class of settlers, in this journal's opinion, although it would be difficult to reject them once they had come this far. The newspaper then prophetically suggested that it would be better to stop the migration at its source. This is precisely what the Canadian government eventually did.

The Sneed party's arrival and entry, once their medical examinations were completed, was noted across western Canada, and there was immediate comment. On the day the party arrived in Winnipeg, Manitoba's provincial capital, a woman from the nearby city of Brandon, who signed herself "An Englishwoman Who Had Lived in Oklahoma," contacted the editor of the *Manitoba Free Press* with her concerns. She began by regretting the invasion of "thousands" of African Americans into Canada. Since she was concerned with the welfare of the country, and had no great interest in Oklahoma's, she was sorry that Canada was being saddled with people that the southern states did not want. It was Canada's misfortune, if not the country's own fault, that it had not yet passed a law barring people of African descent.

Since liberty was not to be confused with license, she continued, one could only enjoy true freedom by being restrained. Yet everyone learned by sad experience — only usually too late. Those who had never lived in an area inhabited by African Americans, and had only been in contact with "well-disposed" blacks, would find the disgust felt toward them hard to understand, she said. Those who did know their habits, however, could only see blacks as "undesirable" — they could never be colonists or settlers. In concluding she argued that, "As negroes flourish in a hot country and do as little work as possible, it is hoped that Jack Frost will accomplish what the authorities apparently cannot."

No doubt because of the interest stirred, when the Sneed party reached Winnipeg the local Manitoba *Free Press* had a reporter waiting at the station. In his article the journalist noted that not one of the 194 African-American homeseekers had been rejected at the border, and indicated that "a good deal of speculation is rife as to the outcome of the new movement." He then gave a brief history of how the group came to Canada.

This reporter then turned his attention to the question of assimilation, conceding that it was generally recognized that the best settlers were those who could easily be incorporated into the population. It was being argued with some truth, he said, that the African Americans must forever be unto themselves, and were therefore not the best class of settlers. As the immigration regulations then stood, "there is absolutely no means by which the better class of negro farmer may be rejected."

A "member of the much maligned and hated race," Samuel H. Gibson, contacted the *Free Press* after this article appeared to thank the newspaper for its "fair, candid, and impartial statement." He wanted to thank them, he said, because as far as he was aware they were the first western Canadian newspaper to get all the facts and to express an "unbiased opinion." He continued by asserting: "Much has been said and written on the matter [African-American immigration], but, for the most part, I opine, it has emanated from persons whose minds are warped by blind prejudice, and who, therefore, are incompetent to sit in judgement on any question of which impartiality is the principal element."

The Edmonton *Journal,* like its Winnipeg counterpart, had a reporter waiting at the station when the Sneed group arrived in that city, indicating once again the importance attached to their appearance. At five o'clock in the morning everyone on the train was very, very tired. Even then the group's spirits were not dampened, and one member of the Sneed party managed to have fun with the reporter. Alighting from the train, one African American announced to the newspaper man that he was so tired that he felt like he was turning yellow. The reporter said he "reeled, staggered, and leaning against the station building felt a little faint at coming on such a supposed revelation." He said that he had heard the expression "yellow coon" used in jest, but never thought that he would come across such a type. Approaching the black jester the journalist was able to see under the station's lights that in fact the African American had not changed colour, and he was able to inform the Oklahoman that "such an affliction had not overtaken him."

Mr. R. Jennings, editor and managing director of the *Journal,* noted that the African-American immigration was causing considerable uneasiness among the whites of western Canada. He did not find this at all surprising: "Whether well-founded or not, we have to face the fact that a great deal of prejudice exists against the coloured man and that his presence in large numbers creates problems from which we naturally shrink." Yet if the African Americans met the existing immigration requirements , in Jenning's opinion, it seemed impossible to deny them entry.

Given these circumstances, the Edmonton journalist continued, one would but wish them well in their new homes, and hope that they conducted themselves so that the ill will directed at them was reduced. They could become useful if they followed Booker Washington's idea of salvation through hard work. There would be plenty of that where they were headed, he concluded, and if they were able to turn their wild land into productive farms they could prove to be more desirable citizens, "than any of those who are now speaking so contemptuously of them and are loafing about the city streets."

Not all Albertans, however, were willing to be quite so liberal. In a front-page news item the Calgary *Herald* informed its readers of the large African-American party's arrival in the provincial capital. They were a much talked-about group, it noted wryly, "heralded throughout their entire journey by more widespread publicity than they would have received had they been the latest thing in a minstrel show." The men were all strong and sturdy, it reported, and the immigration hall in Edmonton was full of "tumbling piccaninnies" which promised another successful generation.

In the same issue the editor of the *Herald* concluded that the African-American immigration was the first fruits of reciprocity with the United States. Canada and the United States were at the time negotiating a free trade agreement, commonly called reciprocity. This journalist saw a connection between these discussions and the arrival of the black farmers. The "colour question" was soon going to agitate the public, and he found Frank Oliver's approach to the question "tepid." It seemed as if the Minister of the Interior was allowing the African-American colony to establish itself, and that he somehow then hoped to sweep them back southward. Teddy Roosevelt's question of what to do with the blacks was being answered, according to this journalist, by sending them to Alberta. "Reciprocity," he concluded, "means that Canada is anxious to take all that America does not want."

The public was already agitated. On 31 March 1911, F.T. Fisher of the Edmonton Board of Trade had penned a seven-page letter to Frank Oliver. Fisher noted that the subject of African-American immigration had been discussed a year earlier by his organization, but that the influx had grown considerably. It was time for "drastic action" since there was evidence that "bitter race prejudice" would develop in the areas where the African Americans were settling. There was no room for argument, and the contention that the African Americans were good people and farmers was irrelevant. One only had to look at the United States to see what would happen if too many blacks came north. He had had white settlers in his office, he said, the very best sort of settler, who would not go to the areas where the African Americans were located. Fisher argued that serious trouble was brewing. In his words,

> White settlers in the homestead districts are becoming alarmed and exasperated and are prepared to go to almost any length. People in the towns and cities... are beginning to realize the imperative necessity of effective action; and it only needs a slight effort to start up an agitation which would be joined in by practically every white man in the country. There is every indication that unless effective action is taken, such an agitation will be put in motion in the near future.

Oliver as already receiving evidence of the racist mood of white western Canada. The secretary of Edmonton's Municipal Chapter of the Imperial Order Daughters of the Empire, a women's patriotic group, forwarded a petition against African-American immigration from her organization to Oliver. She informed the minister that they had held an emergency meeting on 27 March to discuss the black immigration issue, and had decided that they were against it. As if to echo Fisher's claim of possible violence in areas where the African Americans were locating, the Secretary of the Athabasca Landing Board of Trade wrote to Oliver that "When it was learned around town that these negroes were coming out there was great indignation, and many threatened violence, threatened to meet them on the trail out of town, and turn them back." The secretary also said that as there already were African Americans in the area, and only a few whites had as yet located there, there was a danger of the district becoming all black. He suggested that as a remedy the new African-American arrivals be segregated with another group that had already located near Lobstick Lake, west of Edmonton.

For the time being, Sneed's group was unperturbed by the controversy their arrival had created, as they joined one of their preachers in celebrating their apparent good fortune. An African-American minister gathered a group of 75 together in one of the outsheds of the Edmonton immigration hall. Seated on wooden stumps and boxes they heard him say that God had made Canada a free country, but that it was up to them to make the best of it. The reporter covering the event was impressed by the fact that the preacher never mentioned or referred to the United States; he took it to mean that the group was very impressed with what they had seen on the northern side of the international boundary. Their apparent satisfaction was to be short-lived, however, when a tragic accusation further aroused white prejudice in western Canada, and initially reflected upon the entire group and any future African-American settlers.

Shortly after six o'clock on 4 April 1911, 15-year-old Hazel Huff was found by a neighbour lying unconscious on the kitchen floor of her Edmonton home. She had a handkerchief securely tied over her eyes and apparently had been drugged with chloroform. The neighbour immediately contacted a doctor and the police. When the girl regained consciousness she told the police that she had answered a knock at the door, and was grabbed by a black man who tried to drug her. She fought him, she claimed, but was overpowered, and did not remember anything after that point.

When her parents returned home they searched the house and found that a diamond ring and some money were missing. According to one report, the father was so enraged that he took his daughter and his revolver, and went searching the streets of Edmonton for the supposed assailant. The police believed two black men were involved, although they only arrested one: J.F. Witsue. He was charged with robbery two days later, but the police refused to elaborate on the story even when pestered by reporters.

The news of the supposed attack spread as quickly as the proverbial prairie fire, and managed to pick up a few additions on the way. Several newspapers immediately linked the African-American settlers with the incident. The Calgary *Albertan* assured its readers that no criminal assault other than the use of the drug had taken place, and in a later editorial argued that "The assault made by a coloured man upon a little girl in Edmonton should open the eyes of the authorities in Ottawa as to what may be expected regularly if Canada is to open the door to all the coloured people of the republic and not bar their way from open entry here." The Edmonton *Journal* apparently deserted its former moderate stance, since it reprinted this comment in total and with no response. The Calgary *Herald* argued that the attempts to colonize African Americans north of Edmonton had to be carefully examined. The drugging of the girl in Edmonton could be taken as an indication of what could happen in Alberta as a result of African Americans being allowed to settle in Canada.

On Saturday, 8 April, the Lethbridge *Daily News* published an editorial which revealed that the ancient spectre of the "black rapist beast" was still alive in western Canada. Entitled "The Black Peril," this commentary noted that the assault upon the Edmonton girl had come very soon after the arrival of the large party from Oklahoma, and argued that it was a warning to the authorities of what to expect if African Americans were allowed to enter the country. Canada did not need a "negro problem." The blacks who were already in the country had to be kept away from the homesteads, it continued, for in the more isolated areas, where women were often left alone, there would be an ever-present terror. "Keep the black demon out of Canada," was its stand.

This was too much for a local black farmer, L.D. Brower, and he contacted Lethbridge's other newspaper, the *Daily Herald* to reply. After noting the "black peril" comments, Brower attacked the argument it contained. He asked what the paper thought of the immorality of slavery, and whether it knew that black men had defended white women during the American Civil War? The source of the *News'* prejudice was its envy of the progress African Americans had made since 1865, and thus it would deny them the right to freely enter Canada. The Edmonton story was probably a fake, and while waiting for the truth he would farm his land and the blacks further north would tackle the wilderness. The *News,* in the meantime, could continue to supply its form of "intellectual food," but, he said, "I submit to the judgement of the fair minded Canadian citizen, which of us is best improving his God-given talents."

The Saskatoon, Saskatchewan, *Daily Phoenix* announced the incident to its readers in a completely distorted front-page item with a large headline: "A Negro Atrocity — White Girl Flogged and Assaulted by Late Arrivals at Edmonton." It went on to say that the first black atrocity since the large party arrived from the United States ten days before had been reported. The Regina *Leader* carried much the same item on its front page, which prompted a comment from the Edmonton *Bulletin*. Perhaps because of its close association with Frank Oliver, the *Bulletin* had remained strangely silent on the question of African-American immigration in general, and the large Sneed group in particular. The Regina report aroused the *Bulletin*'s editor to state that,

> Bad news not only travels fast, but like a snowball on the down grade the further it goes the bigger it grows. This particular item picked up a second negro and flogging between Edmonton and Regina. It can hardly have been less than a murder and a lynching when it reached Toronto, and a free-for-all race war by the time it got to New York.

Even when it was determined that the man charged had no connection with the Oklahoma settlers feelings against the group in Edmonton remained high. Furthermore, in one journalist's opinion, another such incident would push the "rowdy element" of the city to the lynching point. Even the saner members of the community believed that the black influx had to be stopped. The editor of the Calgary *Herald* commented that the "negro problem" was the most serious then facing the United States. Edmonton had the sympathy and support of the whole west in protesting the African-American immigration, and it was hard to understand Frank Oliver's apathy to the situation.

Taken together, these reports indicate that the age-old sexual mythology surrounding the black man was being reinforced in many white western Canadian minds. Indeed, when Fritz Freidrichs of Mewassin, Alberta, contacted the Canadian immigration authorities on 12 April to voice his disapproval of the African-American immigration, his major concern was that, "These negroes have misused young girls and women and killed them". This was tragic, but the full dimensions of the tragedy were not revealed until nine days after the supposed assault when the young girl confessed to having made up the whole story.

According to the Edmonton *Journal* the young girl "had not been attacked and overcome by a big, burly nigger who was intent on robbing the house, as was first believed." The girl had lost the diamond ring involved and, fearing punishment, had made up the tale. She became frightened with the commotion caused and, when a man was charged, decided to confess. Interestingly, the Edmonton chief of police had known the truth for several days, but had sworn the family to secrecy. No explanation was given for this action.

The girl's story had an impact, before she confessed, and cannot be divorced from the agitation against African-American immigration which continued to grow. On the night of 7 April, Mr. C.E. Simmonds of Leduc addressed a "representative gathering" at the Conservative Party club rooms in Edmonton. After discussing and criticizing the Liberal's reciprocity policy, he turned his attention to the subject of immigration. Just as British Columbia was fighting Oriental immigration, and did not want to be called "Yellow British Columbia," Simmonds said, he did not want his province to be labelled "Black Alberta." It was time immigration reflected personal rights; they all had a right to choose whom they wished to live near. He did not want Alberta to be black, he continued, or even black in spots, and he believed that the province would not stand for a black invasion. "I can see only one way out of this difficulty," he concluded, "and this is to put the present government out of power and bring in one who will listen to our pleas... Way down in Ottawa they do not think of the matter as seriously as we do, and therefore the interest is lacking."

The Edmonton Board of Trade was determined that Ottawa would listen, and it launched a vigorous petition campaign. After giving a brief account of early African-American immigration into Alberta, the board's petition argued that these people were but the advance guard of several more hundreds, and that their arrival would be disastrous. It continued,

> We cannot admit as any factor the argument that these people may be good farmers or good citizens. It is a matter of common knowledge that it has been proved in the United States that negroes and whites cannot live in proximity without the occurrence of revolting lawlessness, and the development of bitter race hatred...We are anxious that such a problem should not be introduced into this fair land at present enjoying a reputation for freedom from such lawlessness as has developed in all sections of the United States where there is any considerable negro element. There is no reason to believe that we have here a higher order of civilization or that the introduction of a negro problem here would have different results.

It was then urged that immediate steps be taken to stop any more African Americans from settling in western Canada.

81

The Edmonton Board set up a special committee to oversee the distribution of the petition throughout the city. Copies were placed in several banks and hotels downtown and in the Board of Trade office, and plans were made to canvass door-to-door. The committee was perhaps spurred by a newspaper report from Vancouver that a Colonel Tom J. Harris of Sapulpa, Oklahoma, was planning to bring more African Americans to Canada. The Kentucky-born "Colonel" was quoted as saying he would bring 5,000 "niggahs" north before the summer ended. Members of Edmonton's City Council may also have seen this item because when a letter from the Board of Trade asking for support was read at a council meeting on 25 April it was immediately acted upon. Only one alderman, Mr. McKinley, voted against endorsing the Board of Trade's action.

The agitation against them must have seemed all too familiar to the African Americans who had recently arrived from Oklahoma. They had moved to that state to escape white racism, only to see it raise its ugly head in the West. They had now moved north to try to escape again, and here was another strain of the white racist virus attacking them. Still, they were not about to submit to it — they had fought before and were ready to fight again. African Americans in Edmonton quickly organized to try to nullify the Board of Trade's petition campaign.

Their tactic was to have several black residents follow a canvasser, interrupt any conversation he might have trying to get signatures, and try to dissuade anyone from signing. They appear to have had some success because Secretary Fisher of the Board of Trade criticized these efforts arguing that the blacks did not "appreciate the spirit" in which the petitioning was being done. The local blacks should recognize that the idea of excluding others was merely an attempt to prevent a repeat of the situation in the United States, and that their own position would be worse with a larger black community. In an only slightly veiled threat Fisher also said, "Those negroes who have been here some time have had a square deal and been treated as whites, but if you would get a few thousand more in, conditions would be much changed. They would then be treated as they were in the south." He also claimed that nearly everyone approached was signing the petition and, while his 95 percent success rate is questionable, over 3,400 Edmontonians eventually did sign.

The Edmonton Board of Trade also had considerable success when it contacted other similar business groups across western Canada. By the end of May, 1911 the Strathcona, Morinville, Fort Saskatchewan, and Calgary Boards of Trade had either endorsed or joined the Edmontonians in urging that the African-American immigration be stopped. They were joined by their counterparts in Yorkton and Saskatoon, Saskatchewan, and Winnipeg, Manitoba.

Other groups and organizations also joined in the racist chorus. On 29 April, Francis C. Clare, Secretary-Treasurer of the Edmonton Chapter of the United Farmers of Alberta, wrote to the federal Immigration Branch to say that his group was "in full sympathy with the resolution passed by the Edmonton Board of Trade." On the same day, J.M. Liddell, Secretary-Treasurer of the Pincher Station, Alberta Chapter of the UFA, also wrote to Ottawa to register his group's disapproval of black immigration, and to urge that they be excluded permanently. In his words, "we consider negroes undesirable as fellow citizens of this Province." The Edmonton Builders Exchange, an organization of many contractors' groups, sent a separate petition calling the African-American migration a "serious menace." A.C. Sawley of the Athabasca Landing Board of Trade wrote to the Minister of the Interior, Frank Oliver, stating, "Canada is the last country open to the white race. Are we going to preserve it for the white race, or are we going to permit blacks free use of large portions of it?"

In Saskatoon, Saskatchewan, the local Board of Trade's endorsement of the Edmonton position brought praise from the local newspaper, the *Daily Phoenix*. The action may seem to have been rather harsh, this journal argued, but it was convinced that it was in the best interests of both Canada and the African Americans. The two races could never have anything in common and, while the coming of a few might be all right, hundreds would be a far more serious matter.

Several days later "Fair Play" contacted the newspaper to challenge this argument. Having lived in a black town this writer felt qualified to speak on the subject. He argued that the blacks could be as good citizens as whites, and included some statistics from a federal Department of Justice report on prison inmate populations to prove his point.

Unfortunately for "Fair Play" the data he cited was open to challenge, as the *Daily Phoenix* noted two days later when an editorial in response to his letter appeared . The statistics proved the opposite, the paper said, since they showed blacks to have a pro-portionately higher inmate population than whites. The *Phoenix* then went on to argue that the "problem of the Negro" on the North American continent was America's, and had no place in Canada. The agitation against the African-American migration was due to the large numbers of Americans living in western Canada for "there is no inherent unfriendliness towards the black man in this country."

This smug Canadian assertion that the racist feelings being voiced in the west were from white American settlers was not new, but it did not go unchallenged. When Estelle Coffee of Neilburg, Saskatchewan, contacted the Edmonton *Journal* at the height of the African-American immigration controversy she asked why "the people of this country accept the negro as their equal socially and object to them as neighbours?" Obviously a former American, this woman attempted to poke a hole in the inflated Canadian claims of racial tolerance, and tried to get them to accept some respon-sibility for the agitation then underway.

This American settler found it hard to understand why the peo-ple of the north who believed, preached, and practised social equal-ity objected to black settlers. It would be easy to understand why a white Southerner would object to living with blacks: "We do not accept them as our equals at any time or in any way." She wanted to know if it was right to keep blacks from settling in Canada when everyone seemed so anxious for them to have every advantage. If Southerners could live with thousands of blacks, she concluded, sure-ly Canadians could tolerate a few hundred.

While white westerners displayed a degree of hypocrisy on the race question, this by no means indicates that other Canadians were somehow free from the taint of racism. Describing blacks as "that special element, the worst of all," Arthur Fortin, LLB, of St. Evarist Station, Beauce, Quebec, contacted Frank Oliver to assure him that any government action to stop the African-American influx would meet with the approval of that part of French Canada. He personally felt that they should try "to prevent or at least control the immigration of Darkies into the Dominion. Just as it does for the Chinies — the Hindoes — and the Japs..."

White immigrant groups in western Canada also sided with the dominant anglophones on the issue. After the Winnipeg Board of Trade passed its resolution on the black immigration question, the German-language *Der Nordwesten* newspaper of that city, after

quoting from the document, argued that

> . . . dass die vielen Faelle von Lynchjustiz im Sueden der
> Staaten, von denen wir fast taeglich lesen, und bei denen
> es sich fast ausschliesslich um Verbrechen handelt, die von
> Negern begangen worden sind, wohl jeden, abgesehen von
> anderen Gruenden, ueberzeugen duerften, wie wenig wuen-
> schenswert ein solcher Zuwachs unserer Bevoelkerung ist.

> Es waere zu wuenschen, dass noch andere offentliche
> Koerperschaften von der Art der hiesign Handelskammer —
> sich dem Protest der letzteren anschliessen.

> [. . .we should like to add that the numerous instances of
> lynch law in the southern states, about which we read almost
> daily and which deal almost exclusively with crimes likely
> each committed by Negroes, these instances should con-
> vince us, apart from other reasons, how undesirable such
> an increase is to our population.

> It would be wished that other public corporate bodies like
> the Board of Trade join in the protest.]

Racial prejudice was brought to western Canada in the minds
of white immigrants. The dominant anglophone groups which
settled in the region had well-developed views of blacks before the
African Americans began arriving from Oklahoma. These prejudices were confirmed, and spread by the local press which
portrayed blacks in a racist manner.

Western Canadian newspapers' coverage of the African-
American migration reinforced these prejudices, and ensured
that when African Americans stepped down from the immigrant
cars they were greeted by a virulent racism unlike that experienced by any other group of settlers. The intensity of the emotion
generated against the African Americans was out of all propor-
tion to their relatively small numbers. The western Canadian reaction was also tinged with a sexual dimension unlike that found in
the reaction to other immigrant groups.

The white western Canadian response to the African Americans
was plain racism. Like their American cousins, western Canadians
had inherited a profound prejudice to dark-skinned peoples, and
did not want to have black neighbours. Like their fellow plains-
men in Oklahoma they were also ready to support government
action to keep the northern plains as white as the annual snow-
falls which covered it.

Chapter Six

CANADA'S DIPLOMATIC RACISM

For a period of one year from and after the date hereof the landing in Canada shall be and the same is prohibited of any immigrants belonging to the Negro race, which race is deemed unsuitable to the climate and requirements of Canada.

— Canada, Order-in-Council,
No. 1324, 12 August 1911.

When the Democratic Party launched its 1910 campaign to deprive Oklahoma's African Americans of their voting rights, more blacks began to appear at the Canadian border. White settlers in western Canada, confronting numbers of prospective African-American neighbours, did not resort to direct violence. They did threaten it, but ultimately turned to government action.

The Canadians were more successful than the Oklahomans in their efforts to keep their region white because they were able to exert pressure on their national government. The provincial governments of western Canada, like their American state counterparts, were closer to the scene of the drama but lacked the ability to act on the issue. Immigration into the country was largely a federal matter. White westerners found that the Government of Canada was of a similar mind on the issue of black immigration, and ready to use the tools at its disposal to prevent more African Americans from entering the country. This was itself a form of violence, because it forced African Americans to continue to live with racist attacks in Oklahoma with little hope of escape.

John and Mildred Ware

"Auntie" and the children of Colonel James Macleod

Government advertising lured thousands to the Canadian plains

Provincial Archives of Manitoba

W. D. Scott

Frank Oliver

Wilfrid Laurier

Mattie Mayes

And it's Too Warm in Dixie

African-American settlers, Amber Valley, Alberta

J. D. Edwards farm, Amber Valley, Alberta

Mabel Lockhart and students

African-American family, Athabasca, Alberta

P. C. 1324

AT THE GOVERNMENT HOUSE AT OTTAWA.

PRESENT:

HIS EXCELLENCY

IN COUNCIL:

His Excellency in Council, in virtue of the provisions of Sub-Section (c) of Section 38 of the Immigration Act, is pleased to Order and it is hereby Ordered as follows:-

For a period of one year from and after the date hereof the landing in Canada shall be and the same is prohibited of any immigrants belonging to the Negro race, which race is deemed unsuitable to the climate and requirements of Canada.

To Interior 15 Aug. 1911

Wilfrid Laurier

approved Grey 12/11 Aug 12/11

The "Deemed Unsuitable" Order-in-Council

Frank Oliver, the federal Minister of the Interior, the ministry responsible for immigration, became so concerned with the developing black exodus from Oklahoma that he sent an employee on a five-day investigation of the situation. The agent reported by letter in September of 1910.

The Canadians then took steps to try to halt the immigration. They contacted their agent in Kansas City, who was closest to the scene, and suggested that he get in touch with the postmasters of the towns stamped on enquiries, asking whether the person writing was black or white. If the agent could find out which writers were black he would send them no immigration literature. Some of the postmasters' replies show the state of race relations in Oklahoma at the time. One reply from Keystone used the term "Nigger," while another from Hominy read, "black as hell."

The border points of Emerson, Manitoba, and Portal, Saskatchewan, were alerted to examine any prospective African-American settler carefully since Canadian immigration agents in the United States had been instructed to no longer issue settlers' certificates to African Americans.

When several African-American families appeared in Edmonton in December of 1910, Oliver wanted to know who had let them in, and whether they had been medically examined. On 5 January 1911 the minister got his answer. This group had gone from Oklahoma to Vancouver, on Canada's west coast, and then up to Edmonton. The government immigration officers in Vancouver were then given the same instructions as those at other border crossings. A telegram to the Edmonton agent on 5 January directed him to take action if he could discover any reason for deporting any of the immigrants. It also suggested that he call in the city health officer if he suspected any of the African Americans of not meeting the physical qualifications for immigration.

Canadian immigration authorities appear to have believed that they could stop the influx by depriving African Americans of information. This was at best haphazard because in Oklahoma at the time there were many ways of finding out about Canada.

The Canadians then tried the deterrent of vigorous medical examinations at the border, and even went so far as to try to bribe their own medical authorities. In the Spring of 1911, the American Consul-General in Winnipeg, John E. Jones, was called on to help a group of his black fellow Americans enter Canada. Jones later determined that a Canadian immigration official in western

Canada had offered a medical inspector a fee for every potential African-American immigrant he turned away. To his credit the doctor does not appear to have taken the money. In any case, tough medical inspections were rendered ineffective when obviously healthy African-American men, women, and children presented themselves at the border.

In March 1911, the physical condition of Henry Sneed's group shattered the medical examination exclusion idea. Their ability to leap the medical barrier, plus their numbers, were two reasons why the Sneed group attracted so much publicity. That publicity provoked comment revealing white western Canadians' deep feelings on the subject of African-American immigration. This widespread public response was soon echoed at the highest levels of government in the northern Dominion.

Canada's government is parliamentary in form, modelled on that of Great Britain. In the United States, the President is both the head of state and the head of the government; in Canada the two functions are split. The reigning British monarch, who is also the King or Queen of Canada, is represented in their North American domain by a Governor-General who serves as the head of state. The head of the government is the Prime Minister, the leader of the party with the most seats in the House of Commons. These seats are filled in periodic national elections.

While the American President is free to choose cabinet members subject only to ratification by Congress, the Prime Minister of Canada chooses a cabinet from his party members who have won election to the House of Commons. These ministers are then responsible to the House for the operations of their departments, and regularly answer questions posed by members of the House. The Canadian Senate is an appointed body whose members are selected, as vacancies become available, by the government at the time. Its role is largely symbolic. Senators review legislation passed by the House of Commons before it goes to the Governor-General for signing into law.

At the time of the African-American migration the Liberal Party, led by Wilfrid Laurier, controlled a majority of seats in the Canadian House of Commons. The Conservative Party, headed by Robert Borden, formed the official Opposition. The Liberals had been in power since 1896, but were facing increasing criticism over their negotiation of a free trade package with the United States.

The Conservatives sought to capitalize on this situation, and were ready to embarrass the ruling party at every opportunity.

Widespread agitation against African-American immigration could not but come to the attention of Parliament, and the subject was raised several times in the House of Commons. Even before the large Sneed party arrived, Frank Oliver was questioned about his department's policies regarding black immigrants. The Minister of the Interior, in a blatant falsehood, assured the House on 2 March 1911 that "there are no instructions issued by the Immigration Branch of my department which will exclude any man on account of his race or colour."

When, a few weeks later, the subject of African-American immigration was again raised, Oliver admitted that there was a strong sentiment against the admission of people of African ancestry, but he assured the House that African Americans seeking to enter Canada would be subject only to the existing provisions regarding immigration.

Robert Borden, the Conservative Party leader and leader of the Opposition, noted that a great deal depended upon how strictly the immigration regulations were applied. He said he thought that it would be unfortunate if anyone were excluded from the country because of their colour. Not all Conservatives were quite so sympathetic, however, and on 3 April 1911, William Thoburn, the Conservative member for the Ontario riding of Lanark North, asked Oliver whether the government was prepared to stop the developing black influx, and whether it would not be preferable "to preserve for the sons of Canada the lands they propose to give to niggers?"

Many white Canadian minds were beginning to link the African-American migration with other "coloured" immigration. On 1 May 1911, William H. Sharpe, the Conservative member for the Manitoba riding of Lisgar, rose to state that, like British Columbians who were concerned with Asian immigration, he wanted a "white West." He urged the government to stop the flow of African Americans.

Clearly, the Canadian government, like many of its western citizens and several members of parliament, did not want African Americans in western Canada. Taking action was proving to be difficult: reciprocity, or free trade, negotiations with the United States had only recently been concluded, and remarks on the issue by President Taft had fanned the fires of Canadian nationalism. A volatile subject such as African-American immigration could easily upset an already precarious situation. Indeed, one Calgary newspaper had already linked reciprocity and black immigration in a very negative fashion.

The American government was likewise concerned with what was happening, but it too faced a delicate situation. Late in April, 1911, the Winnipeg Consul-General, John Jones, was in Washington to discuss the African-American migration issue with the Assistant Secretary of State. Jones presented a memorandum from Winnipeg immigration officials saying Canada might bar African Americans because they could not adapt to the climate, and therefore were liable to become public charges.

Since the United States had itself banned Asian immigration it had little room to maneuver. Given the already strained state of Canadian-American relations, the American State Department did not want to pursue the matter of African-American migration to Canada. In addition, Washington's inability and reluctance to aid black Americans at home was implied by the influential *New York Times* comment on the Oklahoma migration and Canada's reaction to it:

> ...it is necessary to consider the facts as well as the opinions, and with a certain sentiment of toleration and humility. It is difficult to take any high view regarding the inhospitality of Canadians, both citizens and officials toward "nationals" who are fleeing from equal intolerance at home, and ill-treatment at the hands of both neighbors and legislators.

While Canada tried to find a solution to its growing dilemma, events in Oklahoma were forcing even more African Americans to try to escape. In 1911 their situation was becoming all too clear, especially after an ugly lynching in May of that year. An African-American mother and son, arrested for murdering a deputy sheriff, were taken from the Okemah jail by a white mob, dragged to a railway bridge south of town, and hanged.

African Americans in Oklahoma were horror-struck by the event. According to one African-American newspaper, pictures of the bloody crime were being openly sold. This journal did not attempt to conceal its anguish when it cried:

> Oh! where is that christian spirit we hear so much about—
> What will the good citizens do to apprehend these mobs —

Wait, we shall see —- Comment is unnecessary. Such a crime is simply Hell on Earth. No excuse can be set forth to justify the act.

Western Canada still offered an escape from these horrors. Despite its concern with African-American immigration the Canadian government had not removed its advertisements from African-American newspapers in Oklahoma. Throughout 1911 the qualities of the northern plains continued to be described in glowing terms. The Canadian authorities were also well aware of the continuing interest of African-American Oklahomans. On 14 March 1911, the Secretary of the Department of the Interior alerted the Deputy Minister that "if we are to prevent a large influx of these people during the next six months, some steps will have to be taken at once."

Another measure of continued African-American interest in moving to Canada was the commentary offered in the black Oklahoma press. Most African-American editors felt that their people should stay where they were and face their problems. The Clearview *Patriarch*, for example, understood that it had cost more than five thousand dollars to transport one large party north. This newspaper argued that such a sum, if added to another, could operate a huge business that would be a "credit to the race." It also did not believe that the best results could be obtained by moving so often.

Another African-American journal was even more emphatic. After noting that many African Americans had come to Oklahoma in the early days, overcome crises, built themselves homes and farms, and now had a place where they could raise their heads, it argued that these same people were now selling everything they had without due consideration. Conditions in Oklahoma were improving, it urged.

Reports of the agitation against the African-American immigration into western Canada obviously buttressed the black editors' arguments. On the front page of its issue of 13 April 1911, the Clearview *Patriarch* reprinted an entire editorial from the Edmonton *Journal* of 27 March that recognized the existence of racist prejudice in western Canada. The *Patriarch* then pointed out that the Canadian item proved that, wherever he went, the black man had to face a problem.

Not quite a month later the African-American newspaper the *Oklahoma Guide* of Guthrie carried a front-page item from an unidentified New York newspaper headlined, "Protest against Immigration — Race Prejudice Caused by Colored People in Canada". This piece noted the increase in racist feeling in Alberta and Saskatchewan because of increasing African-American immigration from Oklahoma, and observed that for the first time since Americans began moving north a class of American citizens was being deemed undesirable by Canada. The resolutions of the boards of trade of Edmonton and other western Canadian communities were reported, as was the argument that blacks could not adapt to the climate. This, the African-American journal suggested, was only a polite way of saying that people of African ancestry were not welcome. The Canadian government was obviously feeling the pressure of public opinion, the newspaper argued, and it could be forced to pass restrictive immigration regulations. American federal authorities were also in a delicate position, wrote the journal: "Although the federal government does not protect the Negro from disfranchisement at the hands of the Southerns, it does hold him entitled to the same rights as the white man under foreign treaties and conventions."

African Americans in Oklahoma continued to be informed of Canada's reception of their brethren. The Muskogee *Baptist Informer* carried an item on 8 June 1911 about a resolution of the Calgary Board of Trade against African-American immigration. But there was a more personal source of information, although it was somewhat biased, for African Americans who were interested in going to Canada or for those who were already headed north. Some time in April or May of 1911 the Canadian federal government sent the first of its agents to Oklahoma to report on the racial situation, and to take action against the African-American migration to Canada. The Canadian government had finally found a way to stop, and not merely frustrate, the black trek.

Sending an agent to Oklahoma was part of a Canadian government plan to stop the African-American migration. In a confidential meeting held on 22 May 1911 the strategy was revealed to John Jones, United States Consul in Winnipeg, by Bruce Walker, the Canadian Commissioner of Immigration in that city. During the meeting Walker stated that an order-in-council barring blacks from entering Canada would shortly be approved. In the meantime, the Government of Canada was doing all that it could to persuade African Americans not to go to western Canada. The agent in Oklahoma, Walker stated, was pointing out to African Americans the trouble they would have with the Canadian climate and the prejudice that was emerging in western Canada against their entry. The agent was suggesting to African-American Oklahomans that they were the innocent victims of a scheme, engineered by a major railroad company operating in Oklahoma, to get their land for less than it was worth by telling them to go to Canada.

Walker also told Jones that he had hired an African-American physician from the United States, and had sent him to investigate the existing African-American settlements in western Canada. Once the doctor had completed his report, it would be sent to Ottawa. In the meantime, the usual medical inspection of immigrants would be dropped for African Americans, Walker indicated, since it was the government's intention to bar them completely.

C.W. Speers was the first agent sent to Oklahoma by the Canadians. He contacted the Inspector of United States Agencies, W.J. White, in Ottawa on 8 May 1911 and again on 17 May to report on his visits to Muskogee, Tulsa, Oklahoma City, and Wellston, Oklahoma. He described the African Americans' poor housing and generally inferior living conditions, and argued that "Jim Crow" segregation and disfranchisement were the "great source" of their problems.

Speers had been able to discuss the immigration issue with several African-American preachers, and said he believed that this was the area with the best potential for stopping the flow. Dr. S.S. Jones, President of the Oklahoma Conference of Black Baptists, and editor of the *Baptist Informer,* had readily agreed with Speers' assessment of the situation and had promised to use his influence to stop more African Americans from leaving. Several of Jones' colleagues had joined him in this vow.

Dr. Jones was as good as his word. He publicized his meeting with Speers and the other African-American church leaders in his newspaper. Speers was correct, the preacher argued, African Americans should stay in Oklahoma and fight for their rights. Jones also wrote to a senior Canadian immigration official — W.D. Scott, Superintendent of Immigration — to inform him that African Americans should not enter Canada because of the harsh climate, and gave the Canadian permission to use his letter in any way he saw fit.

The Immigration Branch became aware of Speers' success on 15 May 1911 when it received a letter from the Reverend H. H. Edmond of Oklahoma City. Edmond contacted Scott for information about Canada before advising his congregation on whether to leave. He was having second thoughts since Speers contacted him, but he wanted to know for certain what the weather and the country were like. Scott replied with a letter arguing that because of the climate Edmond and his African-American followers should not come north.

Speers was in Chicago during the last week of May, 1911, but his interest still lay farther south. On 24 May he addressed virtually identical letters to Dr. Jones and to a Reverend Hernagin in Oklahoma City, following up on earlier contacts. Speers referred to Booker T. Washington's teachings and stated:

> Surely with a degree of confidence they [African-American Oklahomans] can let their buckets down and draw from their own resources in the midst of their own congenial surroundings.

> Why should your people be driven hither and thither, through oppressive and despotic measures to climates and conditions wholly unsuitable? Why cannot they dwell in peace enjoying every privilege of full citizenship in the country and under conditions best suited to themselves?

> I feel assured that your advice to the colored people will not only benefit them, but reflect credit upon yourself.

On 31 May, Speers, now in Ottawa, wrote to W.D. Scott that he had observed the agents of American railroads operating in Oklahoma trying to increase traffic by encouraging African Americans to go to Canada. He had spoken to railroad officials when he was in Kansas City, he said, and they had promised to stop this soliciting.

Speers also indicated that he had spoken to D.B. Hanna, Third Vice-President of the Canadian Northern Railway, when he was in Toronto. Hanna had promised to use his influence on the American railroad companies. Speers then suggested that William Whyte, Second Vice-President of the Canadian Pacific Railway, should also be asked to use his influence "as there is a strong international courtesy between the railway companies. I feel assured that this would have a very good effect."

Speers' success with the African-American clergymen, and his continual references to Booker T. Washington's theories, may have been the basis for a suggestion by W.H. Rogers, now the Canadian agent in Kansas City. In a letter to an unnamed superior in Ottawa, Rogers argued that the only way to stop African Americans from heading north was by striking the fear of death into them. He proposed that evidence on blacks dying in cold climates be collected and sent to Booker T. Washington, who believed that African Americans should stay in the south. "I feel sure his influence would be a material advantage to us in this matter," Rogers concluded.

While there is no evidence that his proposal was ever acted upon, it did reflect a mind fertile with schemes to stop the African-American migration, and it was not Rogers' only proposal. In an earlier letter to the Canadian Superintendent of Immigration, the Kansas City agent had said that he was very pleased with the work Speers had done in Oklahoma, and recommended that he continue it. He felt that Speers' approach was the most effective way of dealing with the problem, but if that agent was unable to return to Oklahoma, a Reverend J.B. Puckett could be used. "This man," Rogers said, "would not cost the Department nearly as much as that coloured man from Chicago."

"That coloured man from Chicago" was Dr. G.W. Miller, an African-American medical doctor who had been hired to tour the black settlements already established in western Canada. Apparently satisfied with his report, the Canadian Government sent Miller as its second agent to try to stop the black trek from Oklahoma. Miller, an African American, was clearly the more effective agent for the Canadians because he was more readily accepted by other blacks. In addition, he had professional medical qualifications, and could therefore lend weight to the idea that African descendants would be affected by Canada's climate.

Exactly when the doctor arrived in Oklahoma is as obscure as how much he was being paid, but beginning on 24 June 1911 he was sending daily reports to Canadian immigration officials in Chicago. In his first report, sent from Muskogee, Miller said that he had interviewed a Reverend Perkins of the Second Baptist Church, and had convinced him to keep his congregation in Oklahoma. In the next day's report Miller said that he had spoken to large audiences at the First and Second Baptist churches, and thought that he had managed to change a number of minds considering leaving for Canada. He also said that he had arranged to have his address printed in Dr. Jones' Muskogee *Baptist Informer.* There was a problem, however, because this time the clergyman-publisher wanted to be paid for the service.

Miller's first two reports were a blueprint for his activities over the next month. He would enter a town or city, contact the African-American clergymen and anyone else he heard was interested in going to Canada, arrange to speak in the churches or at some large gathering, and have his speech reprinted in the local African-American newspaper, if there was one.

Dr. Miller wasted no time for he rapidly criss-crossed eastern Oklahoma. On 26 June 1911 he reported from Okmulgee that he had spoken to several African-American clergymen who had promised to help stop the flow northward. On 27 June he was reporting from Weleetka, having stopped at Bryant and Henryetta en route. He had not found any African Americans planning to emigrate in either of the latter places, but many people in Weleetka seemed interested in going north, and he called a meeting for the next night. "It is quite an easy matter to get the people here," Miller said, confirming white Canadians' worst racist fears, "as they are all anxious to hear about Canada."

On 28 June Dr. Miller described the meeting in Weleetka, and once again claimed to have convinced many black Oklahomans not to head north. He explained that he began his talk by "describing minutely" what happened to him when he entered Canada. He then went on to describe a snow storm he had witnessed, and the early as well as the late frosts he had encountered. He found that these descriptions were new to the Oklahomans. His aim, he explained, was not only to discourage the northward migration, but to get the African Americans to see how thankful they should be to live in Oklahoma, with its bountiful soil and good climate.

Miller was being modest in describing his talks. An article he wrote for the Guthrie *Oklahoma Guide* has survived, and it is possible to gain an insight into his discussions. Dr. Miller's job for the Government of Canada was to counteract their own immigration advertising, and to frighten prospective African-American settlers from leaving for the north country. The article began with a running commentary on what African Americans could expect when reaching Canada, and then singled out specific areas that they would be interested in hearing about. He said that he felt that it was his solemn duty to his race to make them aware of the conditions he found when he travelled in western Canada, and of the plight of those who had already headed north without question or investigation. He could not understand why people would sacrifice what they had spent their lives acquiring, he said, to go to a country "that is desolate, frigid, unsettled, unknown and to which they are climatically unfamiliar and financially unfit."

The African Americans' problems would begin at the international boundary. A Canadian government inspector would meet them, Dr. Miller said, and examine their luggage. He explained, in terms which recalled the bitter memories of slave auctions, that the entire family would be subject to a thorough medical examination "where your wife and daughter are stripped of their clothes before your very eyes and examined by a board of men. What man of you would desire his family undressed and humiliated in such a manner," he asked.

Nor were these the only inspections. Their livestock was also examined, but since this commonly took thirty days the extra expense was a real financial burden. All of this took place, Dr. Miller said, even before they were allowed to enter the "so-called promised land."

The African Americans should not think that they would escape racial prejudice by entering Canada because, according to Dr. Miller, wherever there were two distinct races hostility appeared. Still, there were those who would disregard his warnings, who would rush off and waste their life's savings, and do it all in a land where the winters were long and cold, and the summer "but a dim memory of morning."

Dr. Miller went on to tell black Oklahomans that they should stay where they were; where they had friends, happiness, and bountiful harvests. Besides, their children had to go to school, and there were none in the Canadian woods. If they wanted to go to a city or to church they would have to travel great distances.

They would also have to go at least seventy-five miles to find a doctor, Miller said, whereas in Oklahoma they had medical help at the door. Above all, there was the intense Canadian cold — snow fell waist deep, and the ground froze to a depth of from six to ten feet. They had all been born and raised in the south and, according to Dr. Miller, "it will cost your life to live one winter in Canada."

The Chicago doctor then turned his attention to specific subjects such as food, clothing, the soil, crops, the seasons, water, and shelter, but his overwhelmingly negative tone did not change. They would find that food cost twice as much in Canada as it did in Oklahoma, he said, and because of the climate they would find that they ate more. Their farms would not keep up with their demands, and they would end up buying food imported from the United States. They could not get many of the foods they would want and, if it were true that man lived to eat, then many of them would surely die. If they did not starve, then they would freeze to death or die of consumption or pneumonia because they lacked the proper clothing. After spending all of their money to be transported to their new homes, Dr. Miller argued, they would find that they did not have the funds for the required warm clothing and furs.

Nor was the soil in western Canada what they had been led to believe. It was a sand-based light sod, and anyone with farming experience would know that nothing profitable would grow in it. Their homesteads would be covered with timber and bush, and in every open area grew a vegetable called muskeg. They would need to know scientific farming to raise crops in Canada, Miller argued, because they would have to deal with a killing frost in June and another one in August. Furthermore, there were only two seasons in Canada: winter and summer. The winters were so long, Dr. Miller explained, that they would start to think that summer would never come.

The only houses to guard against the Canadian climate were log cabins, which they would have to build themselves. They would have to fill the cracks with mud, but when it rained the mud would fall out and the cold wind would blow in. As if all this were not bad enough, Dr. Miller said, the only water they could get was a mixture of alkali that would injure their stomachs and make them ill.

Dr. Miller carried his message from Weleetka to Clearview, Oklahoma, and on 29 June 1911 he reported from the latter town that many African Americans there were planning to leave for Canada. He spoke to a large gathering, and arranged to have his address published in the local African-American newspaper. On 30 June he was in the all-black town of Boley speaking to a number of prominent citizens, and was informed that a local movement was underway to try to stop the migration northward. Guthrie was Miller's next stop, and in that town he spoke to several African-American clergymen who arranged for him to speak to a large audience by announcing the meeting in all of the town's African-American churches.

At the gathering Miller's statements were challenged by relatives of settlers already in Canada. Those who had left had written home to say that they were doing well. Miller left the assembly, however, "satisfied that they were convinced that such was not the case."

From 4 July until 8 July Dr. Miller was in Oklahoma City, speaking with families who had expressed an interest in moving to Canada. He again displayed confidence in having persuaded them not to go, but he was not having quite the same success as he had had with the African-American press. Apparently some editors were reluctant to print his article, perhaps because Miller did not wish to have to pay for the publicity.

From 9 July until 11 July he was in Watonga, speaking at churches and interviewing families who were thinking of leaving. Miller reported his usual success, but found that some families were so poor that they did not have the means to leave in any case. Back in Oklahoma City on 12 July he spoke to a few more potential migrants. There he found that some African Americans had already heard unfavourable reports of Canada. Apparently a former African-American settler had returned from Canada spreading "cold winter" stories.

From Oklahoma City Miller proceeded to Bristow, spending two days there convincing nine families not to leave for Canada. From 15 to 17 July he was in Sapulpa, and again found that a returning settler with an unfavourable report had preceded him. In his last report, dated Sapulpa, Oklahoma, 17 July 1911, Dr. Miller stated,

> The Canadian Boom is rapidly dying out, as the unfavourable reports relative to Canada seem to have spread over the entire state. Everywhere I go, people say they have heard of me and the unfavorable report of Canada.

Dr. Miller was correct. For all intents and purposes the African-American migration from Oklahoma to western Canada faded as 1911 progressed. Dr. Miller had done his work very well.

Miller's success at dissuading African-American Oklahomans from migrating was not immediately apparent. Even as he travelled through the state his employers looked for other ways of stopping the trek. One solution was simply to bar blacks from entering Canada. The Calgary *Herald* newspaper had already suggested such a method. Its Ottawa correspondent had noted that a section of the Canadian Immigration Act of 1910 gave the federal government the power, with an order-in-council, to exclude for a period or permanently, any race thought unsuitable to Canada's climate.

The problem with this approach was that it could discourage white Americans from heading north. Indeed, an official of the Canadian Pacific Railway Colonization Department in Chicago had written to Frank Oliver on 28 April 1911 to complain that newspaper reports citing this argument had already prevented some whites from migrating. This did not stop the Minister of the Interior, and on 31 May 1911 he sent a recommendation to the Laurier Cabinet for an order-in-council barring blacks from entering Canada for a period of one year.

The federal cabinet did not approve the order-in-council immediately. There were several arguments against such a drastic step. It could cause stormy diplomatic relations with the United States when the reciprocity issue was still in the air. Also, there was soon to be a federal election, and every vote would be needed. Why alienate the black voters of Nova Scotia and southern Ontario? In addition, fear of scaring off white American immigrants was undoubtedly a powerful argument against the move.

Such was the depth of white Canadian racism that no argument was strong enough to bridge it. On 12 August 1911, the Canadian federal Cabinet in fact approved an order-in-council barring blacks from entering the country:

> For a period of one year from and after the date hereof the land-ing in Canada shall be and the same is prohibited of any immigrants belonging to the Negro race, which race is deemed unsuitable to the climate and requirements of Canada.

This order-in-council was never acted upon, however. It was repealed on 5 October 1911 on the pretext that the Minister of the Interior had not been present at the August meeting. The fact that it was approved at all indicates how serious Canada was about keeping the northern plains white.

The chronology of events involving the order-in-council also suggests that it was a "pocket" order, to be used if Dr. Miller failed in his mission to Oklahoma. The idea was originally suggested in May of 1911, when the physician was touring black settlements in western Canada. It was approved in August when he was still in Oklahoma, and it was repealed in October when his success at stopping the migration was becoming clear.

Some months later, Canadian immigration officials again became concerned with the black immigration issue. In February 1912, word spread that African Americans were once again looking to Canada as a possible haven. Canadian government officials recommended that an agent be stationed in Oklahoma City or in Muskogee to handle the issue, and that legislation be passed barring blacks from entering the country.

The Inspector of United States Agencies for the Government of Canada was in Ottawa on 22 February 1912, writing letters to American railroads (the Soo; the Rock Island; the Missouri, Kansas and Texas; the Frisco; and the Union Pacific lines), asking them not to encourage African Americans to emigrate from the southern United States to Canada. This official told these railroads that he was also contacting the Great Northern, Northern Pacific, and Santa Fe lines on the matter, although no record of this correspondence is in the files of the Canadian Immigration Branch.

The renewed black trek never materialized, and Canadian concern regarding blacks in 1912 was with a number of friends and relatives who were trying to visit settlers already in the country. The Canadian officials' apprehension about these people was expressed in a reply to a question from John Foster, United States Consul in Ottawa, regarding one visiting African American who had been turned back at the border. Foster was told that Canada was concerned that these people were, in fact, trying to settle in Canada, but were entering, "under the guise of tourists or visitors."

Canadians' reaction to the African-American migration indicated that they believed many of the same stereotypes and myths about blacks as did white Americans. While white western Canadians did not resort to direct violence to halt the black trek, they did urge their government to develop policies to stop the African Americans.

Haphazard discrimination against people of African ancestry through medical examinations, and depriving potential black settlers of immigration material were covert and deceptive methods. Sending agents to discourage African Americans from migrating was considerably more successful, and by the autumn of 1911 the black trek from Oklahoma to the Canadian Plains was coming to an end.

Chapter Seven
THE ONGOING STRUGGLE

...if there is a law in this country that does not recognize CREED, COLOUR, OR SOCIAL STANDING you have a chance of showing or proving it to us.
— Letter from the Eldon District
Resident Ratepayers to the
Saskatchewan Deputy Minister of Education,
23 March 1914.

The African Americans who crossed the forty-ninth parallel into western Canada faced not only the usual obstacles and trials associated with pioneer farming, but also the entrenched racial attitudes of their new white neighbours. It was an ongoing struggle, one for which the pattern of their earlier migrations had alerted them.

African Americans who moved north to Canada had been part of the westward migration to what became Oklahoma. They were among the vanguard of those who headed west rather than accept second-class citizenship in the older southern states.

Among Maidstone, Saskatchewan's black settlers, was James G. Gordon, who had been born in Winona, Mississippi; William Crawford who was originally from South Carolina, while Peter Taler was from Georgia. J.C. Lane had been born in Virgina, but his kinsman Walter Lane had been born in Dalbow, Missouri, which would indicate that the Lane family spent some time in that state on their way to Oklahoma.

African-Americans settlers in the Amber Valley district of Alberta, north-east of Edmonton, had also been part of the westward movement in the United States. Jeff Edwards' family moved from Arkansas because they heard there was no segregation in the Indian Territory. Willis Bowen's parents had been slaves, and had moved to what became Oklahoma after Emancipation.

The Bowens were another black family that appears to have moved several times before settling in Canada. Willa Dallard (nee Bowen) had been born in Evergreen, Alabama, on 12 June 1897. The family left Alabama for Wortham, Texas, before moving to Wellston, Oklahoma. They then stayed briefly in Guthrie, Oklahoma, before leaving for Alberta via Bellingham, Washington, and Vancouver, British Columbia. Willa's husband, Noah Robert Dallard, born in Harrisonburg, Virginia, on 12 March 1885, was also part of the westward migration.

Another Alabaman who had moved west before turning north was Essie Matthews Lane, wife of Walter Lane. She had been born in Hillsborough, Lawrence County, Alabama, in 1898. When she was ten years old her grandfather, Lewis Forster, a preacher, moved the family to House Creek, Oklahoma. Just two years later the family was on the train headed to Canada.

The family histories of other African-American migrants to western Canada confirm the pattern of westward movement to what became Oklahoma before the turn north to Canada. Dwight Tyler of Athabasca, Alberta, recalled that his grandfather had moved to the Choctaw Nation where Dwight had been born. Anna Groff of Edmonton, Alberta, said that her father had been born in Joplin, Missouri, and her mother in Smiths Grove, Kentucky. Rosa Shannon's father was raised in Omaha, Nebraska, before he moved to Oklahoma. The Taylor sisters remembered that their mother had been born in Tennesee, and their father in Kentucky. Frank Johnson was born in Dallas, Texas, and had moved to Oklahoma before leaving for Canada. Texaner Jamerson had been married in Texas, her granddaughter recalled. Matilda Payne Allen, who would later settle in Saskatchewan, was born in Birmingham, Alabama. Reddick Carruthers and Henry Sneed were both originally from Texas, had moved to Oklahoma, and later moved to the Amber Valley district of Alberta.

A few black migrants to Canada may have been "black Indians." The Ross family of Breton, Alberta, claim descent from the great Creek chief John Ross, although since Ross was a Cherokee their claim is somewhat suspect. Mark Hooks, also of Breton, is a descendant of a mixed African American and aboriginal family. Willa

Dallard's mother was Jenny Thigpen, who was half-black and half-Cherokee. Some family histories probably laid claim to an aboriginal ancestor so that land could have been obtained in Oklahoma. Surviving evidence indicates that fewer than ten percent of the original migrants to Canada claimed an aboriginal ancestor.

African-American experiences at the Canadian border were hardly necessary to alert them to the struggle ahead. Nor was the commotion their arrival generated in the region's press. The African Americans seem to have deliberately placed themselves well away from more heavily settled areas, possibly to minimize contact with whites. The areas they settled were remote, even by the standards of this settlement era. Black farmers headed to the alternating bush and meadow lands which form the northern boundary of Canada's share of the Great Plains.

Of course there were other factors operating in the choice of a settlement location. The presence of several African-American families near Maidstone, Saskatchewan, may have influenced others to locate in the Eldon district, north of Maidstone. According to local tradition, the African Americans who headed toward Breton, Alberta, south-west of Edmonton, were drawn there by the knowledge that a bush fire had recently raced through the area, and they thought that the land would now be easier to clear.

Nor did the African-American groups disperse once they reached Canada. They chose to settle together in the isolated districts, usually a close walk or easy ride from one another. There were good reasons for staying together. A number of the families were related, and the kinship bonds held tight. In addition, some of the African-American groups had been members of the same congregations in Oklahoma, had moved together, and resurrected their religious ties in their new country. Still other African Americans had come from the all-black or largely black areas of Oklahoma. These black pioneers knew the value of group settlement as a defence against white racism.

Once located upon their land the African-American families set to transforming the bush and meadows into productive farms. It was not easy work, and in addition these farmers had to learn new ways of working the land. The majority of the African Americans had farmed cotton and tobacco in Oklahoma, and had to make the transition to the raising of grain and livestock.

Hard work paid dividends. Within a decade of their arrival the African-American families of Amber Valley, for example, were well established. A 1922 Canadian federal government report on the area north-east of Edmonton noted that

> Fields varying in size from 20 to 80 acres
> are common and many of the older settlers
> are well established. The clearing, in general
> is fairly light and fair progress is being
> made each year by the more enterprising settlers.
> The houses and barns are not pretentious and
> are mostly of log construction. Most of the
> present settlers are negroes. Wheat and oats are
> the staple grain crops grown and it is reported
> that the average yield per acres [sic] of wheat is 20
> to 30 bushels an acre and oats 40 to 50...Mixed
> farming is the popular method, and forage and
> garden crops do well. The usual local market
> is Athabaska and most of the grain is disposed
> of at the elevator there...All things considered,
> the outlook for mixed farming in this township
> is very encouraging.

Like their white counterparts, the black farmers of Western Canada did not spend all their working hours in their fields. Cash was always a problem for pioneer farmers, regardless of their colour, and the African Americans supplemented the family budgets by freighting, lumbering, and working on the railroad lines which began penetrating the region. At Junkins (later known as Wildwood) north-west of Edmonton, the enterprising African-American settlers set up a sawmill which furnished the area with building materials.

Within a few years the African Americans began creating the institutions which gave form to their Canadian communities. By 1916 the black settlers in the Eldon district of Saskatchewan had erected Shiloh Baptist Church. A modest log structure, it served the African-American families of the area until it was abandoned in the 1940s. Its lovely cemetery stands as mute evidence of the struggles and sacrifices of the people who sought a refuge in Canada.

In all pioneer communities another important social institution was the school. A large number of children had made the trek north from Oklahoma. They and brothers and sisters born in Canada soon needed to be educated. The African Americans quickly discovered that they had not completely isolated themselves. Obtaining an education for their offspring brought them into contact with their white neighbours, where they quickly discovered that racially mixed schools were as delicate an issue for whites north of the forty-ninth parallel as it had been for those south of it.

In Campsie, Alberta, north-west of Edmonton, local whites simply barred the area's African-American children from getting an education. One African-American mother reputedly took her children to the local school, but found the doors locked against them. The provincial authorities apparently refused to act, and the discrimination lasted for many years.

Not that all of the segregation was imposed. In 1913 Toles School was built in Amber Valley, an area settled by African Americans. The majority of the school's students were black, as were the various teachers and local trustees. The Amber Valley school later added high school grades so that the area's children did not have to travel to nearby towns to continue their education. This situation lasted until the 1960s.

Just east of Amber Valley the African-American farms neighboured ones settled by Ukrainian and Polish homesteaders. When it came to skin colour these eastern Europeans quickly made it known that they shared the attitudes of the dominant English-speaking groups of the Canadian Plains. The Silver Fox School, which was begun in 1916 and opened in 1917, served this racially mixed area. For years after it was founded the school had difficulty keeping its teachers, supposedly because of the hostile attitudes of the black students. When Mabel Lockhart, a white teacher, arrived at the school in 1931 she quickly determined that the black students' anger was due to the attitudes of the school's white students, who were convinced of their racial superiority and conducted themselves as if the belief were true.

Mabel Lockhart was a gifted teacher fondly remembered by her students decades later. As she recalled,

> In order to combat this concept of white
> supremacy I put forth a special effort to
> impress on all the children that as far as
> colour was concerned I regarded them as equals,
> that behaviour, not colour, was the all
> important factor in assessing true worth. And

> that it was by their behaviour alone that I
> would judge them. In the classroom I made
> certain that every pupil received equal
> attention. Whenever credit was bestowed on a
> white child the same credit was bestowed on a
> black one...whether for effort or achievement.

A far more complex school situation developed in the Eldon district of Saskatchewan. This district stretches along the south bank of the North Saskatchewan River, approximately half way between the cities of Lloydminster, on the Alberta-Saskatchewan border, and North Battleford, Saskatchewan. The area, once part of Cree hunting grounds, had been settled after the turn of the century by British immigrants.

African-American settlers arrived in the district in 1910 and 1911. Once they had established themselves they turned their attention to obtaining a school. By 1913 they had encountered enough difficulties to begin contacting the Saskatchewan Department of Education in the provincial capital of Regina.

African-American settlers' farms were situated within an existing school district, but the school was remote from them. In order to create a new district closer to their property they had to obtain the local municipal council's permission to change the boundaries. According to the provincial legislation then in effect, "Every such application shall set forth clearly and concisely the grounds upon which such application is based and shall be accompanied by a plan showing the proposed alteration...."

The local governing body with which the African Americans had to deal was the Council of the Rural Municipality of Eldon No. 471. This group met on Monday, 10 March 1913, to consider the blacks' petition; they rejected it, arguing that the application"...being found incorrect in form and computation was ordered to be returned to the petitioners." The African Americans tried to correct the application, but this too was rejected. The reason given this second time was that the petitioners were not qualified voters — a rejection undoubtedly hard to accept by people who had only recently left Oklahoma because they had been disfranchised.

This second set-back apparently caused some of the African-American settlers to begin wondering if there was more to the dispute than a simple change in school district boundaries. They persuaded a local teacher to contact the provincial educational authorities on their behalf. The teacher wrote toward the end of June, 1913, outlining the difficulties the settlers had encountered, and concluded that the group deserved the authorities' help because

> most of the people in the district are negroes who have come from the United States. They are a thrifty class and some of them are fairly well educated.

In mid-July the Saskatchewan Department of Education replied, advising the African-American settlers to apply to the council once more; if nothing was then done to contact the Department again. Apparently the Eldon Council did not take any action, because three months later a school inspector was in the area investigating the problem for the Department. The inspector's report was the first indication of the racial basis of the school controversy.

The inspector reported to his superiors in Regina that he had it "on good authority" that the African Americans had applied to the Eldon Council three times, and had been rejected on each occasion. He also noted that, because of these rejections, the African-American settlers were beginning to feel that they were being prevented from forming a school district. He had reported the accusation to a member of the Eldon Council and had been told that the plan would be passed as soon as it came before the council in the proper manner.

Still, the school inspector had his doubts that this would actually happen:

> There is opposition undoubtedly. Some white people residing in the proposed district are averse to the district being formed. If it be true, however, as I heard when in the vicinity that they broke up the formation of a district to the west of them which would have enabled them to be in a district free from negroes, they are not worthy of much pity if they are now trapped.

The school inspector's own veiled racism aside, his observations on the situation in the Eldon district are significant. The African-American settlers wanted a school nearer to their homes. They had drawn up the boundaries for a new district, likely using the provincial Department of Education's guidelines. In order to ensure the financial stability of the proposed district, and to conform to requirements, the African Americans included neighbouring white-owned farms in their proposal.

The white settlers did not want to send their children to school with blacks, and probably pressed their municipal councillors to ensure that it did not happen. The Eldon Council was therefore rejecting every African-American application that contained white-owned farms within its boundaries. The idea seems to have been that when the African-Americans became desperate enough for a school they would themselves submit a plan for an all-black school district, or at least agree to a segregated one, and so solve the white families' problem.

The African Americans were not about to submit to racial segregation and the dispute dragged on for years. At one point they submitted yet another boundaries plan. In an incredible display of bigoted gall the Secretary-Treasurer of the Eldon Council either altered the African-American submission, or drew up a new one, to exclude the white-owned farms. Of course the Eldon Council approved this "revised" plan.

The black settlers protested to the provincial authorities, but shrewdly focused their complaint on the small size of the new district, arguing that it was unlikely to be able to support itself financially. The provincial officials called upon the Eldon Council to explain its actions. On 11 December 1913 the council met, and directed its Secretary-Treasurer to inform the provincial education officials that "the omission of the western row of sections was owing to the fact that this was strictly comprised of white people whereas the suggested area was wholly a coloured population."

With this admission the Eldon Council, and the white settlers it represented, made their position perfectly clear. They would not allow the creation of a racially mixed school district. Racism was at the core of the Eldon district school dispute, and was no different from the racism which the African Americans had fled in Oklahoma.

In their efforts to segregate their black neighbours, the white settlers of the Eldon district enlisted the help of their provincial Member of the Legislative Assembly, Mr. J. P. Lyle. He investigated the dispute, and told the education authorities that "The matter is a very important one, as the settlers are considerably worked up about having to send their children to school with the negroes."

The more he looked into the affair the more Lyle concluded that the African Americans had good reason to complain about how they were being treated. He spoke with some of the black settlers, and came to realize how strongly they felt about what was happening to them. In his words,

> It seems to me that their district is not wide enough, and although it might be better to keep them apart, upon their representation I am led to believe that we are doing them an injustice in treating them differently to any other British subject in the country. They feel this rather keenly, and they say that they are here and that they were brought here by the Government and that they have the same rights as men of other nationalities who are now in this country.

The African Americans also let the provincial Department of Education know their views. They contacted the education officials directly to complain about the Eldon Council's alteration of the district boundaries, and demanded the one they had drawn up. They also dramatically stated that

> If there is a law in this country that does not recognize CREED, COLOUR, or SOCIAL STANDING you have a chance of showing or proving it to us. Now sir we are waiting to hear from you before taking it up with the Department of Education at Ottawa [emphasis in original].

As recent American immigrants the settlers were unaware that there was no federal Department of Education in Canada. What they did know was that they were being discriminated against because of their skin colour. Having left Oklahoma to escape just this sort of racism, they were not about to tolerate it in their new country.

The African-American settlers of the Eldon district continued to make their concerns known to provincial officials. In a later piece of correspondence a spokesperson stated:

I would like to call your attention
to the fact that there are some settlers
in this district trying to discriminate
against others in this district on account
of colour, and we hope that you will raise
yourself above lending aid to any such
movement.

Unfortunately for the African Americans the officials of the Saskatchewan Department of Education were not above aiding segregation. They developed a plan dropping the disputed white-owned farms from the proposed school district, and solving the size problem by adding additional black-owned farms. In effect, they created a larger but still racially segregated school district.

The African Americans protested, but discovered that the Department of Education had the power to impose its solution. When the department proceeded to implement its plan black homesteaders refused to serve as trustees, and a white resident of Maidstone had to be appointed. During August of 1915 the white official adjusted the school district's boundaries to add to its tax base. Eldon School was built in 1915, and opened in 1916. While they initially boycotted the governing body, some African-American parents apparently saw the importance of being involved with running their children's school, and in 1917 two of them were elected trustees. The first teacher at the school was black, and until at least 1919 all of the students were black.

As with so many rural areas across the Great Plains the Eldon district gradually lost its young people to the lure of the cities. As the original black homesteaders passed on, or moved away themselves, white farmers gradually began working the land. Ironically, the racial composition of the Eldon School slowly began to resemble the integrated dream of the original African-American settlers. The school district existed until 1951 when it was consolidated along with other small districts of the area into Lloydminster School Unit Number 60.

The young people of the African-American communities of western Canada began moving to the region's cities because of the limited economic opportunities of the rural areas. By 1975 there was only one black farmer left in the Eldon district of Saskatchewan, and only a few in the smaller communities in Alberta. Amber Valley, Alberta remained the largest of the black communities, but in recent years it too has seen its population decline.

Moving to Edmonton, Lloydminster, and North Battleford increased the by now African Canadians' contacts with whites, and white racism. Racial prejudice was common in the cities of the Canadian Plains during the early decades of the twentieth century, and was expressed in a variety of ways. As early as 1912 black residents of Edmonton were complaining that white barkeepers were "drawing the colour line," and refusing to serve black customers.

As in Oklahoma the most common form of bigotry was economic racism. Construction was one of the few activities open to all colours, and black hands were employed in building Edmonton's historic Macdonald Hotel. Other African Canadians found employment in the packing plants of the region's fledgling meat-processing industry. Those who thought that they had escaped the rigors of freighting discovered that cartage and hauling were open to those of African ancestry. Of course one could always start a business, if one had the means, and a number of black entrepreneurs stepped forward to test their skills in the market place.

As the largest city in the area where most of the African Canadians communities were located, Edmonton hosted the greatest number of black-owned businesses. At one time the city was home to cafes, rooming houses, pool halls, barber shops, tailor shops, grocery stores, and hotels all owned and operated by African Canadians. The economic downturns which preceded and followed World War I affected these businesses as much as those of their white-owned competitors. A number of black entrepreneurs relocated to the United States — but not to Oklahoma. These returnees headed to the west coast, and settled in the Los Angeles area of California.

Other black business owners stayed and persevered. A member of the Lane family, from the Eldon district of Saskatchewan, moved to North Battleford and formed a bus company. Today, Lane buses continue to transport the school children of the community.

Starting a bus company took vision and fortitude in an era when the railroads still carried the majority of the travelling public. Both Canada's major railroads provided regular transcontinental passenger service. African Canadians found that railroading was one of the few industries open to them although it too had its limitations. African Canadians from western Canada found steady employment as porters, but for years the more lucrative and prestigious position of conductor was closed to them. African-Canadian railroad families gradually re-located across the country, and today the descendants of western Canada's black pioneers are found in railroad centres such as Vancouver, Calgary, Winnipeg, Toronto, and Montreal.

Despite persistent racial prejudice the black pioneers and their children quickly identified with their new country. Perhaps there was no better indicator of their allegiance than the readiness with which young African-Canadian men volunteered for the Canadian armed forces when World War I erupted in Europe.

African Canadians have a long and distinguished military history. The oldest black families in Nova Scotia proudly trace their ancestry to African Americans who sought refuge behind the British lines during the American Revolutionary War, and turned to fight alongside the red coats. These black soldiers and their families were evacuated to and given land in what would become Canada when the war ended. When American forces invaded Canada during the War of 1812 "The Company of Coloured Men" was among the reinforcements turning back the invaders during the Battle of Queenston Heights in what is now Ontario. One of the first Canadian winners of the Victoria Cross, the highest military decoration in the British Empire, was William Edward Hall, a black Nova Scotian who won his decoration during the relief of Lucknow, India, in 1857. Martin Delany, born in the United States, lived in Chatham, Ontario, prior to the American Civil War, but returned to the country of his birth and in 1865 became the first black commissioned officer of the United States armed forces.

At the outbreak of the Great War, African Canadians, who sought to add to this valiant history, discovered that their skin colour meant more than their readiness to serve. The United States did not go to war until 1917, but Canada's historic attachment to Britain brought it into the conflict at the beginning. In addition, Canada's military tradition has been one of volunteer service. Yet, when African Canadians stepped into the recruiting centres in 1914 they were told that this would be a "white man's war": Canada did not want a "chequer-board" army.

African Canadians across the country refused to accept this racism. Incredibly, they had to campaign to be allowed to serve. In 1916 the Canadian military authorities relented, but did so in a way which confirmed white prejudices. African Canadians were allowed to join a racially segregated construction battalion. *

While the majority of the volunteers for the "black battalion" came from the African-Canadian communities in Ontario, New Brunswick, and Nova Scotia, the small black communities of the Canadian Plains contributed their share to its ranks. The No. 2 Construction Battalion, Canadian Expeditionary Force, trained in Nova Scotia and left for service in Europe in 1917. It was attached to the Canadian forestry corps, and performed its duties in the Jura Mountain region of France. While the unit itself did not see action some of the men were eventually re-assigned and saw duty in the trenches.

Of the nearly six hundred men who made up the battalion, over one hundred and sixty had come from the United States. Even more African Americans would have served in the Canadian army had it not been for the actions of the Canadian authorities. Officers of the battalion contacted immigration officials in October, 1916 to obtain prior clearance for African Americans wanting to cross the border to enlist. W. D. Scott, who had played a major role in ending the black trek from Oklahoma, was still the guardian of Canada's immigration gates. He advised his political superiors to turn down the request, arguing "I think it would be unwise to allow a lot of coloured men to get a foothold in Canada, even under the guise of enlistment in such a battalion."

Nor was this Scott's only contribution to Canada's war effort. By 1917 heavy volunteer enlistment had created a labor shortage in western Canada. There was a desperate need for harvest help, because the foodstuffs produced on the Canadian Plains were a mainstay of the allied war effort. Reports of the labour shortage reached the United States, and on 15 March 1917 a Texan contacted the Canadian immigration authorities with an offer to recruit African Americans as harvesters for Canada. Even though labour needs were serious, Scott appeared to be determined to keep the Canadian Plains as white as the Oklahoma counties which had earlier barred black harvesters. Replying to the American nine days

---

* The story of this military organization is found in Calvin Ruck, *The Black Battalion, 1916-1920*. Halifax: Nimbus Publishing, 1987.

later, Scott coolly summarized white Canadian racial attitudes:

> I do not think it advisable to offer
> any encouragement [to migrate] to coloured
> people in the South, or anywhere else, and I
> regret being unable therefore to take
> advantage of your offer of cooperation.

In both Canada and the United States one effect of the Great War was the growth of urban areas. African-Canadian veterans returning from service overseas joined their white comrades-in-arms in building new lives in the city. For the blacks and their families the transition was not always an easy one because of continuing white racism.

In Calgary, Alberta, in 1920 the white residents of Victoria Park, a neighbourhood just south-east of the downtown core, vigorously protested the "invasion" of "coloured people" into that area of the city. They hired a lawyer, and obtained an emergency meeting with Mayor R. C. Marshall and two city commissioners. According to the Calgary *Herald,* one member of the residents' group bluntly asked whether the city was prepared to buy up properties in the area already owned by African Canadians so that they would all be induced to leave. Mayor Marshall, with equal frankness, said that such a proposal was impossible. He was, however, sympathetic to the residents' concerns. He pointed out that for every black person buying property there was a white person selling it. The Mayor then suggested that

> one of the best methods of preventing
> like trouble in the future was to get
> after real estate men who make such
> transfers under subterfuge, and that an
> aroused public opinion on such actions
> would accomplish more than any move the
> city authorities could make.

The Mayor of Calgary also revealed that civic officials were finding it difficult to direct African Canadians to any part of the city. White Calgarians generally were raising the same objections as the Victoria Park residents to having black neighbours. The meeting adjourned after a decision to have a committee of black representatives meet with a similar body of whites to try to reach a settlement.

Calgary was not the only city on the Canadian Plains, or in the country, to experience problems with race and residence at this time. According to a circular sent to all border inspectors of the western region in the summer of 1920, Canadian immigration authorities were continually receiving reports of African Americans settling in the "undesirable sections" of Canada's cities and towns. The ever vigilant immigration officials informed their front-line employees that

> the Dep't. does not encourage the immigration of colored persons to this country, and further, that none should be admitted who cannot comply with the regulations.

> Some inspectors seem to be under the impression that if a colored person is an American citizen, and appears to be in good health and has the required amount of money, he must be admitted. A strict examination, however, Will [sic] often reveal some statutory cause for rejection....

The summer of 1920 was a busy one in Canada's white immigration officials' struggle to limit the number of blacks entering the country. No sooner had their circular been sent out than another black immigration project was reported. According to the Winnipeg *Free Press* of 1 August 1920, an African-Canadian clergyman from Edmonton was on his way to a black convention in New York where he intended to promote African-American migration to the Peace River district of northern Alberta. Nothing came of this proposal, although Canada's immigration authorities collected an impressive file of newspaper clippings on the organization sponsoring the New York convention.

The organization attracting all this Canadian attention was the Universal Negro Improvement Association (UNIA). The UNIA had been founded by Marcus Garvey, a Jamaican living in the United States. Whites considered it a radical group because it promoted pride in their African heritage among blacks around the world. The UNIA also established black-operated businesses, and encouraged blacks to patronize one another's establishments.

This message of pride and self-help was well received in the African-Canadian communities on the Canadian Plains. After all, these communities owed their existence to these same values. Chapters of the UNIA operated in most of Alberta's black communities during the 1920s.

As justifiably proud as they were of their accomplishments the African-Canadian communities of the Canadian Plains faced a difficult dilemma. In order to maintain their identity they had to grow, but their young people were leaving for the cities. One solution to the problem was to encourage more people of African ancestry to move to the Canadian Plains. With that end in mind, in 1923 the Alberta Negro Colonization and Settlement Society was formed, with offices in Edmonton. The aim of the organization was to colonize and settle people of African ancestry on farms in Alberta. The group claimed to have the support of a majority of the province's African Canadians. It was also ambitious and focused.

The Alberta society intended to start their project by recruiting five hundred African-American farmers as the advance guard of thousands more who would follow. Using the African-American press to spread the message, they planned to recruit in Nebraska, Iowa, Illinois, Kansas, and Oklahoma. Each prospective recruit had to possess between $1,500 and $5,000 in order to qualify. Recruits would be settled upon land purchased by the Society in settlements within forty or fifty miles of Edmonton.

Canadian immigration authorities responded quickly to what they perceived as another racial migration threat. Early in 1923 a Canadian agent in the United States met with a spokesman of the Alberta group. He immediately warned his superiors in Ottawa that "the facts in this case present a very serious situation and immediate action should be taken to deal with the matter."

The Canadians did move with haste, and within days sent the following press release over the American wire services:

> Officials of the Department of
> Immigration and Colonization when
> shown a dispatch from Washington to
> the effect that a considerable movement
> of southern negroes to Western Canada
> might be encouraged by the Canadian
> Government, said that they had no
> knowledge of any such movement. While
> Canada is desirous of receiving a

considerable number of farm settlers
it is pointed out that climatic
conditions in the Dominion are such as
to appeal to the white races only. The
suggestion that Canada is likely to make
an appeal for Negro immigration is dismissed
as a pure fabrication.

Recognizing that their project was jeopardized by the racist attitudes of the Canadian authorities a leader of the Alberta society appealed to their "humanitarian spirit." In a letter this spokesman noted that when African Americans had come north over a decade earlier many of them were delayed at the border for "unreasonable causes." He asked that agents of his organization be stationed at the border crossings to prevent a repetition of such incidents.

The Canadian immigration official replying to this plea was the one who three years earlier had instructed western region border agents to search the regulations for reasons to reject prospective African-American immigrants. This official wrote the African-Canadian immigration promoter that having the society's agents at the border stops was against government policy. Perhaps forgetting his own earlier instructions to the border agents this bureaucrat also wrote:

I regret that you seem to think there has
been discrimination against your race in the past.
Will you allow me to say that I am not aware of a
single case of discrimination, of the kind you
mention, within this district.

The actions of the Canadian immigration officials were once again effective, and the plans of the Alberta society to replenish the black communities were halted. Without an influx of new families these settlements, like many of their white counterparts, gradually withered as populations shifted to the cities. This demographic change was accelerated by World War II, a conflict in which African Canadians again served their country.

While the rural African-Canadian communities of the Canadian Plains declined in numbers their fears of a corresponding loss of identity have proven to be groundless. Traditional organizations such as the church have flourished in the cities. As well, new secular groups have been developed to keep alive the memories and ambitions of the original pioneers.

The Shiloh Baptist Church of Edmonton, founded in 1910, continues to serve the city's African-Canadian population. For decades it has been a refuge for blacks who continued to face the racism of their white neighbours. As one parishioner phrased it, "we had to bond together and the church helped us form a brotherhood."

Western African Canadians have developed other organizations as the need arose. In 1960 there were three branches of the Alberta Association for the Advancement of Colored People, Edmonton, Calgary, and Athabasca, with a combined membership of one hundred and fifty. In recent years Canadian communities and ethno-cultural groups have felt a growing need to preserve and communicate their past. African Canadians on the Canadian Plains have responded in several ways. The Black Cultural and Research Society of Alberta was formed in Edmonton to preserve the history of the province's African Canadians. This organization has diligently recorded the reminiscences of both the pioneers and their descendants. It has also publicized the personal and photographic histories of Alberta's black families. Recently, a descendant of one of these families published her autobiography, which chronicled her search for her family's origins. *

There has also been activity in the original rural settlements. In Breton, Alberta, the descendants of the district's black pioneers joined their white neighbours to produce an award-winning local history. **

In 1988 the Amber Valley Community Association received a grant from the Alberta Department of Tourism, Parks, and Recreation to construct a community museum honouring the first settlers of the area.

The African Americans migrated to the Canadian Plains seeking refuge from the white racism they had known in the United

---

* Velma Carter and Wanda Leffler Akili, *The Window of Our Memories*. Edmonton: B.C.R. Society of Alberta, 1981; Cheryl Foggo, *Pourin' Down Rain*. Calgary: Detrelig Enterprises, 1990.

** Breton and District Historical Society, *The Ladder of Time: A History of Breton and District*. Edmonton: Cooper Press, 1980.

States. They headed north from Oklahoma to a region both different yet tragically familiar. They had to learn new ways of farming and how to deal with different government structures. Unfortunately, they also encountered another variety of the white racism from which they had fled. Their ongoing struggle for equality and respect has been taken up by their descendants who now have an historical legacy to call upon as they continue to fight the white racist virus which plagues them.

Changing the World

We must become the change
we wish to see in the world.
— Mahatma Gandhi

Before the outbreak of the American Civil War a woman named Mattie was born in the state of Georgia. Following that upheaval she moved with her family to Tennessee, where in time she met and married Joe Mayes, a Baptist preacher.

Within a decade Mattie and Joe were headed west to the area then known as the Indian Territory to settle along House Creek, near Edna, in what would later become the state of Oklahoma. There Joe became the head of a small Baptist congregation, and also farmed to support their growing family. Presumably Mattie filled the time-honored role of farm wife and mother.

By 1909 Mattie and Joe had heard of good land being available north of the international border on the Canadian Plains. For a ten-dollar fee you could homestead a quarter section and, providing you lived on it for three years and made improvements, the land would become yours. They discussed the idea of moving north with their family and with the members of Joe's congregation, numbers of whom decided to join the trek.

The migrants took wagons to Tulsa, Oklahoma, and then caught a train north. Changing trains in St. Paul, Minnesota, they headed to Winnipeg, Manitoba, and in February or March, 1910, they arrived in North Battleford, Saskatchewan. They stayed at the Immigration Hall, studied maps and weighed possible homesteads. They chose the Eldon district, fifty miles north-west of North Battleford, and eighteen miles north of Maidstone, along the North Saskatchewan River.

The land they chose was not easy to farm. Some of it had to be cleared of bush, and the tough plains sod had to be broken for crops. The new fields had to be regularly planted and harvested, animals tended, and buildings erected. Hard word paid dividends.

121

By the 1920s their farms were well established.

A church, constructed in 1912 of hand-hewn logs covered with wooden shingles, became a focal point for the community. Joe Mayes became the first preacher of the new congregation. In 1913 the first baptism was held at a nearby lake, and the first funeral was held in the little cemetery next to the church.

The growing number of children pressed the Oklahomans to look into developing a school district. Joe was one of the community leaders dealing with the problems of getting one established. These were eventually overcome, and in 1915 the Eldon School was built. It opened in 1916 and the school served the area until 1951 when it was consolidated along with other small schools in the area into a larger school unit.

Mattie left the Eldon district in 1950 to live with one of her sons in Edmonton. She passed away there in 1953. She was buried near the Alberta capital, and not in the Eldon cemetery as she had hoped.

Mattie and Joe's son George stayed in Saskatchewan. His son, Murray, opened an automobile body shop in North Battleford. Murray's family grew, and are now found across Canada and the United States.

Murray's son Reuben became an outstanding football player, and went on to become a Rookie of the Year in the National Football League. He played with the New Orleans Saints, and later with the Seattle Seahawks. He also obtained a degree in administration, and currently operates a job placement service in the Seattle area.

Reuben's brother Christopher also obtained a degree in administration. He is currently working with his father in the family business. Their sister, Lucille, manages a restaurant in North Battleford.

The other sisters in the family have taken on a variety of challenges. Lisa is a high school teacher in Vancouver, British Columbia. Mary Ann has chosen a career in nursing. Chrystal's choice is for a career in the Royal Canadian Mounted Police. Charlotte completed her doctorate in veterinary medicine at the University of Saskatchewan.

The Mayes' story is a familiar one across the Canadian Plains, although the star family athlete usually goes off to play hockey instead of football. The first and second generations in Canada established and developed the family farms, while the third generation moved away to the towns and cities. The fourth generation is now obtaining professional training, and is scattering across the country.

The Mayes' story appears to be exceptional only because of the family's origins in the United States. Canadians are more used to stories of families on the Canadian Plains which trace their beginnings to eastern Canada, Britain, or Europe. Mattie and Joe Mayes were definitely Americans, having been part of the great westward movement of the late nineteenth century which did so much to define their nation.

Upon closer examination this family's American roots are not so unusual. Contrary to popular opinion settlers from the United States were the single largest group to farm the Canadian Plains. They came from across the United States, upwards of three-quarters of a million of them, and they homesteaded and purchased large tracts of land. They broke the sod, established their farms, and joined with their new Canadian neighbours in creating a distinct regional society. They also organized churches and schools, and their descendants are now creating the groups which help to preserve the region's past.

What also appears to set the Mayes family apart is their complexion. Mattie, Joe, and their offspring are the descendants of Africans who were forcibly relocated to North America. Still, this distinctive trait is more apparent than substantial because skin colour is merely a climatic adaptation which our ancestors underwent in different parts of the world.

What is truly unique about this family, and the other African Americans who moved to the Canadian Plains, is the response to their appearance by their fellow North Americans on both sides of the forty-ninth parallel. That reaction is important. That response was racism – the belief that because of their biological inheritance certain people are somehow an inferior type of humanity.

The racist response to the African-American migrants insured that there would be only a few dark complexions in the region during the settlement era on the Canadian Plains. There should have been many more. Black Oklahomans demonstrated that they were interested in settling north of the forty-ninth parallel, but turned elsewhere when it became obvious that the Canadian immigration gates were closed to them.

Such a conclusion is supported by evidence from Oklahoma. In 1913, just two years after the end of the migration to Canada, the same counties of the state which had earlier sent African

Americans north were swept by a "back to Africa" movement. This campaign was led by a native African, Alfred Sam, who toured the Oklahoma countryside selling shares in a trading company which he owned. The shares were a down payment for ship passage back to Africa. Sam was immediately labeled a "con man" by whites and some elements of the black business community, but that did not convince his thousands of followers. *

A thousand African Americans attended a meeting Sam held in Weleetka, Oklahoma in October, 1913. Another large meeting held in the same town in December attracted thousands, and $10,000 was raised to charter a ship. A vessel was contracted from New York, and over five hundred people moved from Oklahoma to Galveston, Texas, to await its arrival. In the meantime, a large tent city developed in Weleetka where many more desperate refugees waited to hear about the outcome of the venture. A small party was actually sent to West Africa to investigate settlement opportunities, but was detained there when World War I erupted. They eventually returned to the United States, but war-time restrictions on shipping effectively ended the movement.

Thousands of African Americans in Oklahoma were willing to sacrifice their money and time on a "back to Africa" movement. Many of them would likely have come to the Canadian Plains if they had not been restricted. The racist policies of the Canadian federal government at the time, supported by the white population of the country and of the Canadian Plains region, ensured that the complexion of their country's immigration would only begin to change decades later.

The reaction to the African Americans illustrates that white Canadians suffered from the same racist myths as their white American cousins. White Canadians believed that the sons and daughters of Africa, like other dark-skinned peoples they knew, were inferior to them. They did not want such people in their communities, or near to them. Whites on the Canadian Plains did not resort to violence to enforce their beliefs. They did, however, threaten such violence and may well have resorted to it if the threat they perceived had not disappeared so quickly. In any case the racism

---

* The full story of this movement is covered in, W.E. Bittle and G. Geis, *The Longest Way Home: Chief Alfred C. Sam's Back-to-Africa Movement.* Detroit: Wayne State University Press, 1964.

displayed on the northern and southern plains was the same, even if expressed differently. Canadians proved to be "polite racists," but racists nonetheless.

Hundreds of miles, and decades of historical development, separate the northern and southern plains regions of North America. When confronted with the prospect of black neighbours, white settlers in both areas reacted much the same. They grasped whatever means were available to them to stop African Americans from living among them.

The reason for the similar reactions lies in the historical origins of the two regional societies. However much they try to prove that they are different from Americans, English-speaking Canadians share a common British inheritance with their southern cousins. However much they try to assert their uniqueness as a people, Americans cannot separate themselves from their British legacy. That inheritance includes a racist element which has remained remarkably consistent through centuries, in very different social situations, and in varying environments.

The white, English-speaking people of the North Atlantic have a long history of racism directed against dark-skinned people. The elements of that racism were present in British society even before the ancestors of Americans and Anglo-Canadians first encountered the peoples of Africa. Through the centuries these elements coalesced into a profound racial bias that ensured that when small groups of African Americans headed to western Canada to escape its effects, they encountered another variation of the same virus, a disease that continues to plague North American society to this day.

The longevity and adaptability of racism casts considerable doubt on the argument that it is essentially an economic phenomenon. Such explanations border on economic determinism. While economic conditions affect the ebb and flow of racial feelings, they are not the root cause. The African-American migration to the Canadian Plains stands as evidence against the economic origins of racism. The movement took place during a period of relative economic prosperity on North America's Great Plains, certainly when the Canadian Plains were flourishing economically. White settlers on both sides of the border still voiced racially based objections to black settlement in their areas of the continent.

The deep roots of white racism also suggest that they will not be unearthed easily, nor quickly. Elements of European racism go back centuries, and some supposedly modern stereotypes appear to have originated in the early Christian era. It will take a great deal more than pious sermons, limp laws, or lame lectures to even begin to dislodge racism from modern society.

In an increasingly interconnected and interdependent world racism is not a belief or attitude that cannot be allowed to continue to poison social relations. As current events continue to remind us, hatred toward others because of their genetic background is too deadly a passion to leave unchecked. While there is no single, obvious prescription for the disease, three things do appear to be needed to begin to eradicate it: time, education, and research.

Racism will not be killed quickly. It is a belief and an attitude which has thrived for centuries. It may take centuries to eliminate it. Such a conclusion offers little solace to racism's victims, nor for that matter to its perpetrators. Social change happens slowly but it does take place, and we have already made great strides against the racist virus. Those engaged in the struggle should not despair at the apparent lack of progress, or the backsliding that regularly occurs. As the great Civil Rights anthem advises, "We shall overcome, some day."

If time is an ally in the campaign against racism, then education is the strategy. What sets humanity apart from other species is its ability to learn, to adjust, and to pass knowledge along to future generations. We have already learned a great deal about racism and its effects. That knowledge must continue to be widely transmitted, not narrowly confined to formal educational environments: schools and colleges. The media, museums, galleries, and other public organizations have a duty and a responsibility to present to their audiences the information on racism which has so far been accumulated.

Ammunition for the educational campaign against racism will come from research. As much as we know about the origins, spread, and impact of racial attitudes we need to know more. *Deemed Unsuitable* has been an attempt to present previously unknown facts about racism to the public. It is the author's fervent hope that if this work does nothing else it will stimulate others to investigate other elements of our racist heritage. If the past sits like a dead weight on the mind of the present — and current racial attitudes offer many poignant examples that it does — then the only way to lift the burden is to continue to study that past.

BIBLIOGRAPHY

PRIMARY SOURCES
Canada
Alberta
    Glenbow-Alberta Institute (Calgary)
    F.F. Parkinson File
    Negroes in Alberta File

Manitoba
    Manitoba Archives (Winnipeg)
    Winnipeg Board of Trade Collection

Ontario
    Public Archives of Canada (Ottawa)
    Department of the Interior Records (Microfilm)
    Privy Council Records

Saskatchewan
    Rural Municipality of Eldon, Number 471 (Maidstone)
    Council Minutes

    Saskatchewan Archives Board (Regina)
    Department of Education Collection
    Oral History Collection

    Saskatchewan Archives Board (Saskatoon)
    Homestead Files

United States
Oklahoma
    Archives of Oklahoma (Oklahoma City)
    Governors' Papers
    Secretary of State Files

    Oklahoma Historical Society (Oklahoma City)
    Clippings Files
    Williams Papers

GOVERNMENT PUBLICATIONS

Canada

Canada. Department of the Interior. Topographical Survey of Canada. *Report on Athabaska District, Alberta, 1922.*

Canada. Parliament. House of Commons. *Debates.*

Canada. Parliament. House of Commons. *Sessional Papers.*

Canada. *Statutes of Canada.* 9-10 Edward VII.

Census of Canada, 1911.

Census of Canada, 1921.

Saskatchewan. Department of Education. *Information Respecting the Organization of School Districts.* Regina, Saskatchewan, 1914.

United States

Fourteenth Census of the United States Taken in the Year 1920.

Proceedings of the Constitutional Convention of the Proposed State of Oklahoma Held at Guthrie November 20, 1906-November 16, 1907. Muskogee, Oklahoma, n.d.

Thirteenth Census of the United States Taken in the Year 1910.

Twelfth Census of the United States Taken in the Year 1900.

United States. Congress. House of Representatives. U.S. Bureau of Refugees, Freedmen, and Abandoned Lands. *Report of the Commissioner.* House Ex. Doc. No. 70, 39th Congress, 1st sess. 1866.

United States. Congress. Joint Committee. Joint Committee on Reconstruction. *Report.* 39th Congress, 1st sess., 1866.

United States. Congress. Joint Committee. Joint Select Committee to Inquire Into the Condition of Affairs in the Late Insurrectionary States. *Report.* 42nd Congress, 2nd sess., 1872.

United States. Congress. Senate and House of Representatives. *An Act to Enable the People of Oklahoma and the Indian Territory to Form Constitution and State Government and be Admitted into the Union.* 59th Congress, 1st sess., 1906.

NEWSPAPERS

Canada
Calgary, Alberta *Albertan.*
Calgary, Alberta *Eye-Opener.*
Calgary, Alberta *Herald.*
Edmonton, Alberta *Bulletin.*
Edmonton, Alberta *Capital.*
Edmonton, Alberta *Journal.*
Emerson, Manitoba *Journal.*
Lethbridge, Alberta *Herald.*
Lloydminster, Saskatchewan *Times.*
Regina, Saskatchewan *Leader.*
Saskatoon, Saskatchewan *Phoenix.*
Winnipeg, Manitoba *Free Press.*
Winnipeg, Manitoba *Tribune.*

Great Britain
The Times

United States
Blackwell, Indian Territory *Times Record.*
Boley, Oklahoma *Beacon.*
Boley, Oklahoma *Progress.*
Cherokee, Indian Territory *Messanger.*
Clearview, Indian Territory *Tribune.*
Clearview, Oklahoma *Patriarch.*
El Reno, Indian Territory *News.*
Guthrie, Oklahoma *Oklahoma Guide.*
Guthrie, Oklahoma *Leader.*
Lexington, Indian Territory *Leader.*
Muskogee, Oklahoma *Baptist Informer.*
Muskogee, Oklahoma *Cimeter.*
Muskogee, Oklahoma *Phoenix.*
Muskogee, Oklahoma *Search Light.*
Muskogee, Oklahoma *New -State Tribune.*
Muskogee, Indian Territory *Western World.*
New York Times.
New York *Tribune.*
Okemah, Indian Territory *Independent.*
Okemah, Oklahoma *Ledger*
Oklahoma City, Oklahoma *Capitol Hill News.*

Oklahoma City, Oklahoma *Oklahoman.*
Sturm's Oklahoma Magazine.
Taklequah, Indian Territory *Cherokee Advocate.*
Vinita, Oklahoma *Chieftain.*
Waurika, Oklahoma *News.*

OTHER CONTEMPORARY SOURCES

Canada
Chambers, E.J. Ed. *The Canadian Parliamentary Guide, 1910.* Ottawa, Ontario, 1910.

Drew, B. Ed. *The Refugee: Or, The Narratives of Fugitive Slaves in Canada.* Boston, 1856. Reprinted, Toronto, 1972.

United States
Ameringer, O. *If We Don't Weaken.* New York, 1940.

Bassett, J.S. *The Southern Plantation Overseer: As Revealed in His Letters.* Northampton, Massachusetts, 1925. Reprinted, New York, 1968.

Blake, W.O. *History of Slavery and the Slave Trade.* Columbus, Ohio, 1860.

Blockson, C.L. *The Underground Railroad: First-Person Narratives of Escapes to Freedom in the North.* New York, 1987.

Bontemps, A., Ed. *Great Slave Narratives.* Boston, 1969.

Botkin, B.A., Ed. *Lay My Burden Down: A Folk History of Slavery.* Chicago, 1945.

Bruce, H.C. *The New Man: Twenty-nine Years a Slave, Twenty-nine Years a Free Man.* New York, 1895. Reprinted, New York, 1969.

Buckingham, J.S. *The Slave States of America.* N.p., 1842. Reprinted, New York, 1968.

Chesnut, M.B. *A Diary From Dixie.* Edited by B.A. Williams. N.p., 1905. Reprinted, Boston, 1949. Revised and reprinted, C.V. Woodward, Editor. *Mary Chesnut's Civil War.* New Haven, Connecticut, 1981.

Cobb, T. *Law of Negro Slavery in the United States of America.* N.p., 1858. Reprinted, New York, 1968.

Donnan, E., Ed. *Documents Illustrative of the History of the Slave Trade,* 4 Volumes. N.p., 1930-1935.

Douglass, F. *Life and Times of Frederick Douglass.* N.p., 1892 Reprinted, New York, 1962.

Higginson, T.W. *Army Life in a Black Regiment.* N.p., 1870. Reprinted, Lansing, Michigan, 1960.

Myers, R.M., Ed. *The Children of Pride: A True Story of Georgia and the Civil War.* New Haven, Connecticut, 1972.

Olmstead, F.L. *Journey in the Seaboard Slave States.* N.p., 1856. Reprinted, New York, 1968.

Osofsky, G., Ed. *Puttin' On Ole Massa.* New York. 1969.

Reid, W. *After the War: A Tour of the Southern States, 1865-1866.* Reprinted, New York, 1965.

Schurz, C. *Speeches, Correspondence and Political Papers,* October 20, 1852 - November 16, 1870. Ed. by F. Bancroft. New York, 1913.

Trowbridge, J.T. *The South: A Tour of its Battlefields and Ruined Cities.* Hartford, Connecticut, 1866.

SECONDARY SOURCES: BOOKS

Canada

Abella, I. and Troper, H. *None Is Too Many: Canada and the Jews of Europe, 1933-1948.* Toronto, 1982.

Adachi, K. *The Enemy That Never Was: A History of the Japanese Canadians.* Toronto, 1976.

Archer, J.H. *Saskatchewan: A History.* Saskatoon, Saskatchewan, 1980.

Bicha, K.D. *The American Farmer and the Canadian West, 1896-1914.* Lawrence, Kansas, 1968.

Breton and District Historical Society. *The Ladder of Time: A History of Breton and District.* Edmonton, Alberta, 1980.

Brown, R.C. *Canada's National Policy, 1883-1900: A Study in Canadian – American Relations.* Princeton, New Jersey, 1964.

_____. *Robert Laird Borden: A Biography*, Volume 1, 1854-1914. Toronto, 1975.

Carter, S. *Lost Harvests: Prairie Indian Reserve Farmers and Government Policy.* Montreal, 1990.

Carter, V. and Akili, W.L. *The Window of Our Memories.* St. Paul, Alberta, 1981.

Clairmont, D.H. and Magill, D.W. *Africville: The Life and Death of a Canadian Black Community.* Toronto, 1974.

Creighton, D.G. *Canada's First Century, 1867-1967.* Toronto, 1970.

Ferguson, T. *A White Man's Country: An Exercise in Canadian Prejudice.* Toronto, 1975.

Fogo, C. *Pourin' Down Rain.* Calgary, Alberta, 1991.

Forsythe, D., Editor. *Let the Niggers Burn.* Montreal, 1971.

Friesen, G. *The Canadian Prairies: A History.* Toronto, 1984; and Lincoln, Nebraska, 1984.

Granatstein, J.L. and Hillmer, N. *For Better Or For Worse: Canada and the United States to the 1990s.* Toronto, 1991.

Hansen, M. and Brebner, J.B. *The Mingling of the Canadian and American Peoples.* Toronto, 1940; and New Haven, Connecticut, 1940.

Henry, F. *Forgotten Canadians: The Blacks of Nova Scotia.* Don Mills, Ontario, 1973.

Hill, D.G. *The Freedom Seekers: Blacks in Early Canada.* Agincourt, Ontario, 1981.

Holmes, J.W. *Life With Uncle: The Canadian – American Relationship.* Toronto, 1981.

Killian, C. *Go Do Some Great Thing: The Black Pioneers of British Columbia.* Vancouver, British Columbia, 1978.

MacEwan, G. *John Ware's Cow Country.* Edmonton, Alberta, 1960.

McKague, O., Editor. *Racism in Canada.* Saskatchewan, 1991.

Morton, W.L. *The Kingdom of Canada: A General History From Earliest Times.* Toronto, 1963 and 1969.

Palmer, H., Editor. *Immigration and the Rise of Multiculturalism.* Toronto, 1975.

_____, with Palmer, T. *Alberta: A New History* Edmonton, Alberta, 1990.

_____. *Land of the Second Chance: A History of Ethnic Groups in Southern Alberta.* Lethbridge, Alberta. 1972.

_____. *Patterns of Prejudice: A History of Nativism in Alberta.* Toronto, 1982.

Ruck, C.W. *The Black Battalion, 1916-1920: Canada's Best Kept Military Secret.* Halifax, Nova Scotia, 1987.

Schull, J. *Laurier: The First Canadian.* Toronto, 1965.

Sharp, P. *The Agrarian Revolt in Western Canada: A Survey Showing American Parallels.* St. Paul, Minnesota, 1948. Reprinted, New York, 1971.

Thomson, C.A. *Blacks In Deep Snow: Black Pioneers of Canada.* Toronto, 1979.

Troper, H. *Only Farmers Need Apply: Official Canadian Government Encouragement of Immigration from the United States, 1896-1911.* Toronto, 1972.

Tullock, H. *Black Canadians: A Long Line of Fighters.* Toronto, 1975.

Walker, J.W. St. G. *A History of Blacks in Canada: A Study Guide for Teachers and Students.* Ottawa, Ontario, 1980.

Ward, W.P. *White Canada Forever: Popular Attitudes and Public Policy Toward Orientals in British Columbia.* Montreal, 1978.

Winks, R. *The Blacks in Canada: A History.* New Haven, Connecticut, 1971.

Wise, S.F. and Brown, R.C. *Canada Views the United States: Nineteenth Century Political Attitudes.* Toronto, 1967.

Great Britain and Europe

Barzun, J. *Darwin, Marx, Wagner: Critique of a Heritage.* New York, 1941 and 1958.

Bolt, C. *Victorian Attitudes to Race.* London, 1971.

Davidson, B. *The African Slave Trade, Precolonial History 1450-1850.* Boston, 1961.

Davis, D.B. *The Problem of Slavery in Western Culture.* Ithaca, New York, 1966.

_____. *The Problem of Slavery in the Age of Revolution 1770-1823.* Ithaca, New York, 1975.

_____. *Slavery and Human Progress.* Ithaca, New York, 1984.

Haller, Jr., J.S. *Outcasts From Evolution: Scientific Attitudes of Racial Inferiority 1859-1900.* New York, 1971.

Himmelfarb, G. *Darwin and the Darwinian Revolution.* New York, 1959 and 1962.

Houghton, W.E. *The Victorian Frame of Mind, 1830-1870.* New Haven, Connecticut, 1957.

Irvine, W. *Apes, Angels, and Victorians: Darwin, Huxley, and Evolution.* New York, 1955.

Kiernan, V.G. *The Lords of Human Kind: European Attitudes to the Outside World in the Imperial Age.* Harmondsworth, England, 1969 and 1972.

Macfarlane, A.D.J. *Witchcraft in Tudor and Stuart England.* New York, 1970.

Mannix, D.P. and Cowley, M. *Black Cargoes: A History of the Atlantic Slave Trade, 1518-1865.* New York, 1961 and 1965.

Marshall, P.J. and Williams, G. *The Great Map of Mankind: British Perceptions of the World in the Age of Enlightenment.* London, 1982.

Notestein, W. *The English People on the Eve of Colonization, 1603-1630.* New York, 1962.

Pei, M. *The Story of Language.* New York, 1949 and 1965.

Russell, J.B. *The Devil: Perceptions of Evil from Antiquity to Primitive Christianity.* Ithaca, New York, 1977.

_____. *Satan: The Early Christian Tradition.* Ithaca, New York, 1981.

_____. *Lucifer: The Devil in the Middle Ages.* Ithaca, New York, 1984.

Shakespeare, W. *The Tragedy of Othello: The Moor of Venice.* Edited by G.L. Kittredge. Waltham, Massachusetts, 1966.

Tawney, R.H. *Religion and the Rise of Capitalism.* Hammondsworth, England, 1922 and 1969.

Trevor-Roper, H.R. *The European Witch-Craze of the Sixteenth and Seventeenth Centuries and Other Essays.* New York, 1967.

Walvin, J. *Black and White: The Negro and English Society 1555-1945.* London, 1973.

Williams, E. *Capitalism and Slavery.* London, 1964.

Woods, W. *A History of the Devil.* New York, 1975.

United States

Aldrich, G. *Black Heritage of Oklahoma.* Edmond, Oklahoma, 1973.

Allport, G.W. *The Nature of Prejudice.* New York, 1954 and 1958.

Andrews, J.C. *The South Reports the Civil War.* Princeton, New Jersey, 1970.

Aptheker, H. *American Negro Slave Revolts.* New York, 1969.

_____. *Nat Turner's Slave Rebellion.* New York, 1966.

_____. *To Be Free: Studies in American Negro History.* New York, 1948 and 1968.

Bennett, Jr., L. *Before the Mayflower: A History of the Negro in America, 1619-1964.* Baltimore, 1961 and 1964.

Berwanger, E.H. *The Frontier Against Slavery: Western Anti-Negro Prejudice and the Slavery Extension Controversy.* Urbana, Illinois, 1967 and 1971.

Bilson, T.B. *The Black Codes of the South.* University, Alabama, 1965.

Bittle, W.E. and Geis, G. *The Longest Way Home: Chief Alfred C. Sam's Back-to-Africa Movement.* Detroit, Michigan, 1964.

Blassingame, J.W. *The Slave Community: Plantation Life in the Antebellum South.* New York, 1972.

Bryant, Jr., K.L. *"Alfalfa Bill" Murray.* Norman, Oklahoma, 1968.

Burbank, G. *When Farmers Voted Red: The Gospel of Socialism in the Oklahoma Countryside, 1910-1924*. Westport, Connecticut, 1976.

Carrol, J.C. *Slave Insurrections in the United States, 1800-1865*. N.p., 1938. Reprinted, New York, 1968.

Channing, S.A. *Crisis of Fear: Secession in South Carolina*. New York, 1970.

Clinton, C. *The Plantation Mistress: Women's World in the Old South*. New York, 1982.

Conway, A. *The Reconstruction of Georgia*. Minneapolis, Minnesota, 1966.

Cornish, D.T. *The Sable Arm: Negro Troops in the Union Army, 1861-1865*. New York, 1956 and 1966.

Cox, L. and Cox, J.H., Ed. *Reconstruction, The Negro, and the New South*. New York, 1973.

Cox, L. *Lincoln and Black Freedom: A Study in Presidential Leadership*. Columbia, South Carolina, 1981.

Crockett, N.L. *The Black Towns*. Lawrence, Kansas, 1979.

Cronon, E.D. *Black Moses: The Story of Marcus Garvey and the Universal Negro Improvement Assocation*. Madison, Wisconsin, 1962.

Cruden, R. *The Negro in Reconstruction*. Englewood Cliffs, New Jersey, 1969.

Dale, E.E. and Wardell, M.L. *History of Oklahoma*. New York, 1948.

Debo, A. *And Still the Waters Run: The Betrayal of the Five Civlized Tribes*. Princeton, New Jersey, 1940 and 1972.

Draper, T. *The Rediscovery of Black Nationalism*. New York, 1969 and 1970.

DuBois, W.E.B. *Black Reconstruction*. Philadelphia, n.d. Reprinted, New York, 1935.

_____. *The Gift of Black Folk*. New York, 1970.

_____. *The Souls of Black Folk*. New York, 1970.

Durden, R.F. *The Grey and the Black: The Confederate Debate on Emancipation*. Baton Rouge, Louisiana, 1972.

Eaton, C. *The Growth of Southern Civilization, 1790-1860.* New York, 1961.

Elkins, S. *Slavery.* Chicago, 1959 and 1968.

Evans, W.M. *Ballots and Fence Rails: Reconstruction on the Lower Cape Fear.* New York, 1966, 1967, and 1974.

Fischer, L.H., Editor. *Oklahoma's Governors, 1907-1929: Turbulent Politics.* Oklahoma City, Oklahoma, 1981.

Fite, G.C. *The Farmers' Frontier, 1865-1900.* New York, 1966.

Fogel, R.W. and Engerman S. *Time On the Cross: The Economics of American Negro Slavery,* two volumes. Boston, 1974.

Foner, E. *Nothing But Freedom: Emancipation and Its Legacy.* Baton Rouge, Louisiana, 1983.

_____. *Reconstruction: America's Unfinished Revolution, 1863-1877.* New York, 1988.

Foreman, G. *A History of Oklahoma.* Norman Oklahoma, 1942.

_____. *The Five Civilized Tribes.* Norman, Oklahoma, 1934.

Franklin, J.H. *From Slavery to Freedom: A History of Negro Americans.* New York, 1947-1956, and 1967.

Franklin, J.L. *Blacks in Oklahoma.* Norman, Oklahoma, 1982.

_____. *Journey Toward Hope: A History of Blacks in Oklahoma.* Norman, Oklahoma, 1982.

Frazier, E.F. *Black Bourgeoisie.* New York, 1962.

_____. *The Negro Church in America.* New York, 1963.

_____. *The Negro Family in the United States.* Chicago, 1939, 1948, and 1966.

Frederickson, G.M. *The Black Image in the White Mind: The Debate on Afro-American Character and Destiny, 1817-1914.* New York, 1971.

Friedman, L.J. *The White Savage: Racial Fantasies in the Post-bellum South.* Englewood Cliffs, New Jersey, 1970.

Genovese, E.D. *Roll, Jordan, Roll: The World the Slaves Made.* New York, 1972 and 1974.

_____. *The Political Economy of Slavery.*
New York, 1965.

_____. *The World the Slaveholders Made.*
New York, 1969.

Gerteis, L.S. *From Contraband to Freedman: Federal Policy Toward Southern Blacks, 1861-1865.* Westport, Connecticut, 1973.

Gibson, A.M. *Oklahoma: A History of Five Centuries.* Norman, Oklahoma, 1965 and 1981.

Gittinger, R. *The Formation of the State of Oklahoma.* Norman, Oklahoma, 1939.

Goble, D. *Progressive Oklahoma: The Making of a New Kind of State.* Norman, Oklahoma, 1980.

Gossett, T.F. *Race: The History of an Idea in America.* New York, 1963 and 1965.

Green, D.E., Editor. *Rural Oklahoma.* Oklahoma City, Oklahoma, 1977.

Green, J.R. *Grass-Roots Socialism: Radical Movements in the Southwest, 1895-1943.* Baton Rouge, Louisiana, 1978.

Gutman, H.G. *The Black Family in Slavery and Freedom, 1750-1925.* New York, 1976.

Handlin, O., Editor. *Immigration As A Factor in American History.* Englewood Cliffs, New Jersey, 1959.

_____. *Race and Nationality in American Life.* Garden City, New York, 1957.

Harris, S.H. *Paul Cuffee: Black America and the African Return.* New York, 1972.

Harris, W.C. *Presidential Reconstruction in Mississippi.* Baton Rouge, Louisiana, 1967.

Hernton, C. *Sex and Racism in America.* New York, 1965.

Herskovits, M.C. *The Myth of the Negro Past.* Boston, 1941 and 1958.

Hofstadter, R. *Social Darwinism in American Thought.* Boston, 1944 and 1955.

Jordan, W. *White Over Black: American Attitudes Toward the Negro, 1550-1812*. Baltimore, 1968.

Kirwan, A.D. *Revolt of the Rednecks: Mississippi Politics, 1876-1925*. New York, 1951 and 1965.

Lewinson, P. *Race, Class, and Party: A History of Negro Suffrage and White Politics in the South*. New York, 1965.

Litwack, L. *Been In The Storm So Long: The Aftermath of Slavery*. New York, 1979.

_____. *North of Slavery: The Negro in the Free States, 1790-1860*. Chicago, 1961.

McPherson, J.M. *The Negro's Civil War*. New York, 1965.

McReynolds, E.C. *Oklahoma: A History of the Sooner State*. Norman, Oklahoma, 1954.

Mead, M. and Baldwin, J. *A Rap On Race*. Philadelphia, 1971.

Meier, A. *Negro Thought In America, 1880-1915: Racial Ideologies in the Age of Booker T. Washington*. Ann Arbor, Michigan, 1963 and 1970.

Miller, J.C. *The Wolf By The Ears: Thomas Jefferson and Slavery*. New York, 1977.

Montagu, A. *Men's Most Dangerous Myth: The Fallacy of Race*. New York, 1964.

Morgan, E.S. *American Slavery American Freedom: The Ordeal of Colonial Virginia*. New York, 1975.

Mullin, G.W. *Flight and Rebellion: Slave Resistance in Eighteenth-Century Virginia*. New York, 1972.

Nash, G.B. *Red, White, and Black: The Peoples of Early America*. Englewood Cliffs, New Jersey, 1974.

_____ and Weiss, R., Editors. *The Great Fear: Race in the Mind of America*. New York, 1970.

Newby, I.A. *Jim Crow's Defense: Anti-Negro Thought in America, 1900-1930*. Baton Rouge, Louisiana, 1965.

Nolen, C.H. *The Negro's Image in the South: The Anatomy of White Supremacy*. Lexington, Kentucky, 1968.

Oakes, J. *The Ruling Race: A History of American Slaveholders.* New York, 1982.

Painter, N.I. *Exodusters: Black Migration to Kansas after Reconstruction.* New York, 1977.

Quarles, B. *The Negro in the Civil War.* Boston, 1953.

Randel, W.P. *The Ku Klux Klan: A Century of Infamy.* Philadelphia, 1965.

Ransom, R.L. and Sutch, R. *One Kind of Freedom: The Economic Consequences of Emancipation.* Cambridge, England, 1977.

Rawly, J.A. *Race and Politics: "Bleeding Kansas" and the Coming of the Civil War.* Philadelphia, 1969.

Redkey, E.S. *Black Exodus: Black Nationalist and Back-to-AfricaMovements, 1890-1910.* New Haven, Connecticut, 1969.

Rice, L.D. *The Negro in Texas, 1874-1900.* Baton Rouge, Louisiana, 1971.

Roark, J. L. *Masters Without Slaves: Southern Planters in the Civil War and Reconstruction. New York, 1977.*

Rogin, M.P. *Fathers and Children: Andrew Jackson and the Subjugation of the American Indian.* New York, 1975.

Schwartz, B.N. and Disch, R. , Editors. *White Racism: Its History, Pathology, and Practice.* New York, 1970.

Scott, A.F. *The Southern Lady: From Pedestal to Politics, 1830-1930.* Chicago, 1970.

Sellers, J.B. *Slavery in Alabama.* University, Alabama, 1950 and 1964.

Sochen, J. *The Unbridgeable Gap: Blacks and Their Quest for the American Dream, 1900-1930.* Chicago, 1972.

Stampp, K.M. *And The War Came: The North and the Secession Crisis, 1860-1861.* Chicago, 1950 and 1964.

_____. Ed. *The Causes of the Civil War.* Englewood Cliffs, New Jersey, 1959.

_____. *The Era of Reconstruction, 1865-1877.* New York, 1965.

_____. *The Peculiar Institution*. New York, 1956.

Stanton, W. *The Leopard's Spots: Scientific Attitudes Towards Race in America, 1815-1859*. Chicago, 1960.

Staudenraus, P.J. *The African Colonization Movement, 1816-1865*. New York, 1961.

Stember, C.H. *Sexual Racism: The Emotional Barrier To An Integrated Society*. New York, 1976.

Sydnor, C.S. *Slavery in Mississippi*. New York, 1933.

Tannenbaum, F. *Slave and Citizen: The Negro in the Americas*. New York, 1946.

Taylor, J.G. *Louisiana Reconstructed, 1863-1877*. Baton Rouge, Louisiana, 1974.

Taylor, O.W. *Negro Slavery in Arkansas*. Durham, North Carolina, 1958.

Tolson, A.L. *The Black Oklahomans, A History: 1541-1972*. New Orleans, Louisiana, 1966 and 1972.

Trelease, A.W. *Reconstruction: The Great Experiment*. New York, 1971.

_____. *White Terror: The Ku Klux Klan Conspiracy and Southern Reconstruction*. New York, 1971.

Voegeli, V.J. *Free But Not Equal: The Midwest and the Negro During the Civil War*. Chicago, 1967.

Wade, R.C. *Slavery in the Cities: The South 1820-1860*. London, England, 1964.

Washington, N.J. *Historical Development of the Negro in Oklahoma*. Tulsa, Oklahoma, 1948.

Wharton, V.L. *The Negro in Mississippi, 1865-1890*. New York, 1965.

White, H.A. *The Freedmen's Bureau in Louisiana*. Baton Rouge, Louisiana, 1970.

Wilson, B.R., Compiler. *Directory and Manual of the State of Oklahoma*. Oklahoma City, Oklahoma, 1967.

Wood, P.H. *Black Majority: Negroes in Colonial South Carolina*. New York, 1974.

Woodson, C.G. *A Century of Negro Migration.* Washington, D.C., 1918.

Woodward, C.V. *Origins of the New South, 1877-1913.* Baton Rouge, Louisiana, 1951.

_____. *Reunion and Reaction: The Compromise of 1877 and the End of Reconstruction.* New York, 1951 and 1956.

_____. *The Strange Career of Jim Crow.* London. England, 1955 and 1966.

_____. *Tom Watson: Agrarian Rebel.* New York, 1938.

ARTICLES, DISSERTATIONS, AND UNPUBLISHED SOURCES

Canada

Avery, D.H. "Canadian Immigration Policy and the Alien Question, 1896-1919: The Anglo-Canadian Perspective." Ph.D. Dissertation. University of Western Ontario, 1973.

Calliste, A. "Blacks On Canadian Railways," *Canadian Ethnic Studies.* 20 (1988): 36-51.

_____. "Sleeping Car Porters in Canada: An Ethnically Submerged Labour Market," *Canadian Ethnic Studies.* 19 (1987): 1-20.

Edwards, J. "History of the Colored Colony of Amber Valley." 21 December 1970. Unpublished paper in the author's possession.

Grow, S. "The Blacks of Amber Valley — Negro Pioneering in Northern Alberta." *Canadian Ethnic Studies* 6 (1974): 17-38.

Johnston, T.F. "Black Canadian Factionalism, Organization, and Militancy." *Review of Ethnology* 6(N.d): 89-101.

Hill, Judith. "Alberta's Black Settlers: A Study of Canadian Immigration Policy and Prejudice." M.A. Thesis. University of Alberta, 1981.

Lockhart (Garrett), E. "One School, One Teacher: Memories of Silver Fox." Unpublished paper, Ontario Institute for Studies in Education, University of Toronto, 30 April 1986.

Palmer, H. and Palmer, T. "Urban Blacks in Alberta". *Alberta History.* 20 (1981):8-18.

Scott, Jr., N.P. "The Perception of Racial Discrimination by Negroes in Metropolitan Winnipeg, Manitoba, Canada." Ph.D. Dissertation. Pennsylvania State University, 1971.

Troper, H. "The Creek-Negroes of Oklahoma and Canadian Immigration 1909-1911." *Canadian Historical Review* 53 (1974): 272-88.

Williamson, D.T. "The Red, White Man." 30 March 1976. Unpublished paper in the author's possession.

Great Britain and Europe
Heather, P.J. "Color Symbolism." *Folklore* 49 (1948): 165-331.

Lorimer, D.A. "British Attitudes to the Negro, 1850-1870." Ph.D. Dissertation. University of British Columbia, 1972.

Spidle, J. "Victorian Juvenilia and the Image of the Black African." Unpublished paper delivered at the Rocky Mountain Social Sciences Association Conference, April, 1973.

Puzzo, D.A. "Racism and the Western Tradition." *Journal of the History of Ideas* 25 (1964): 579-86.

United States
Andrews, J. C. "The Confederate Press and Public Morale." *Journal of Southern History* 32 (1966): 445-65.

Andrews, T.F. "Freedmen In Indian Territory: A Post-Civil War Dilemma." *Journal of the West* 4 (1965): 367-76.

Arnez, N.L. and Antony, C.B. "Contemporary Negro Humor as Social Satire." *Phylon* 29 (1968): 339-46.

Bauer, R. and Bauer, S. "Day to Day Resistance to Slavery." *Journal of Negro History* 27 (1942): 318-419.

Bicha, K.D. "The American Farmer and the Canadian West, 1896-1914: A Revised View." *Agricultural History* 38 (1964): 43-46.

Burbank, G. "Agrarian Radicals and Their Opponents: Political Conflict in Southern Oklahoma, 1910-1924." *Journal of American History* 58 (1971): 5-23.

Chafe, W.H. "The Negro and Populism: A Kansas Case Study." *Journal of Southern History* 34 (1968): 402-19.

Clark, B. "Delegates to the Constitutional Convention." *Chronicles of Oklahoma* 48 (1970/1971): 400-15.

Crowe, C. "Tom Watson, Populists, and Blacks Reconsidered." *Journal of Negro History* 55 (1970): 99-116.

Dann, M. "From Sodom to the Promised Land: E.P. McCabe and the Movement for Oklahoma Colonization." *Kansas Historical Quarterly* 40 (1974): 370-78.

Dickson, Jr., B.D. "The 'John and Old Master' Stories and the World of Slavery: A Study in Folktales and History." *Phylon.* 35 (1974): 481-429.

Fleming, W.L. "'Pap' Singleton, The Moses of the Colored Exodus." *American Journal of Sociology* 15 (1909/1910): 61-82.

Franklin, V.P. "Slavery, Personality, and Black Culture — Some Theoretical Issues." *Phylon* 35 (1974): 54-63.

Friedman, L.J. "The Search for Docility: Racial Thought in the White South, 1861-1917." *Phylon* 31 (1970): 313-23.

Graham, D. "Red, White and Black: An Interpretation of Ethnic and Racial Attitudes of Agrarian Radicals in Texas and Oklahoma, 1880-1920." Master's Thesis, University of Saskatchewan, Regina Campus, 1973.

Hamilton, K.M. "Townsite Speculation and the Origin of Boley, Oklahoma." *Chronicles of Oklahoma* 55 (1977): 180-89.

Hawkins, H.C. "Trends in Black Migration from 1863 to 1960." *Phylon* 34 (1973): 140-52.

Henry, H.M. *The Police Control of the Slave in South Carolina.* Ph.D. Dissertation. Vanderbilt University, 1914. Reprinted, New York, 1968.

Higgins, B.D. "Negro Thought and the Exodus of 1879." *Phylon* 32 (1971): 39-52.

Hill, M.C. "The All-Negro Society in Oklahoma." Ph.D. Dissertation. University of Chicago, 1946.

Hines, L.O. and Jones, A.W. "A Voice of Black Protest: The Savannah Men's Sunday Club, 1905-1911." *Phylon* 35 (1974): 193-202.

Homes, W.F. "Whitecapping: Agrarian Violence in Mississippi, 1902-1906." *Journal of Southern History.* 35 (1969): 165-85.

Littlefield, Jr., D.F. and Underhill, L.E. "Black Dreams and 'Free' Homes: The Oklahoma Territory, 1891-1894." *Phylon* 34 (1973): 342-57.

Meier, A. and Rudwick, E. "The Boycott Movement Against Jim Crow Streetcars in the South, 1900-1906." *Journal of American History* 55 (1968/1969): 756-75.

Meredith, H.L. "Agrarian Socialism and the Negro in Oklahoma, 1900-1918." *Labor History* (1970): 277-84.

Miller, F.J. "Black Protest and White Leadership: A Note on the Colored Farmers' Alliance." *Phylon* 33 (1972): 169-74.

Norris, M.M. "An Early Instance of Nonviolence: The Louisville Demonstrations of 1870-1871." *Journal of Southern History* 32 (1966): 487-504.

Prucha, F.P. "Andrew Jackson's Indian Policy: A Reassessment." *Journal of American History* 56 (1969/1970): 527-39.

Tolson, A.L. "The Negro in Oklahoma Territory, 1889-1907: A Study in Racial Discrimination." Ph.D. Dissertation. University of Oklahoma, 1966.

Wax, D.D. "Negro Resistance to the Early American Slave Trade." *Journal of Negro History* 51 (1966): 1-15.

Weisbroad, R.G. "The Back-to-Africa Idea." *History Today* 18 (1968):30-38.

Wilson, R.A. "Negro and Indian Relations in the Five Civilized Tribes from 1865 to 1907." Ph.D. Dissertation. Iowa State University, 1949.

Woods, R.B. "Integration, Exclusion, or Segregation? The `Color Line' in Kansas, 1878-1900." *Western Historical Quarterly* 14 (1983): 181-98.

Wynes, C.E. "The Evolution of Jim Crow Laws in Twentieth Century Virginia." *Phylon* 28 (1967): 416-25.

Wynne, L.N. "Brownsville: The Reaction of the Negro Press. *Phylon* 33 (1972): 153-60.

NEWSPAPER AND MAGAZINE ARTICLES

Bruns, I. "Kind Hearts and Gentle People." *Montreal Family Herald,* 25 June 1959.

Clark, R.C. "Oklahoma's Northwest Frontier." *Orbit Magazine,* 30 January 1972.

Liddell, K. "New Promised Land." *Saturday Night,* 4 July 1950.

Raugust, P. "Canada — The Canaan to the North for American Negroes." *The Calgary Herald Magazine,* 16 August 1974.

Sessing, T.W. "How They Kept Canada Almost Lily White." *Saturday Night,* September, 1970.

INDEX

A

acculturation, 12-13
African-American Independent
    Suffrage League, 30
African-American Protection
    League, 30
Alberta Association for the
    Advancement of Colored People,
    119
Alberta Negro Colonization and
    Settlement Society, 117
Amber Valley, Alberta, 63, 102,
    104, 106

B

Baptist Informer, Oklahoma, 93, 96
Black Cultural and Research
    Society of Alberta, The, 119
Boley, Oklahoma, 32, 33
Borden, Robert, 88, 89
Bryan, William Jennings, 02

C

Calgary, Alberta, 115-16
    Board of Trade, 92
    see also, Marshall, R. C.
Calgary Herald, 76
Canada,
    immigration, 63, 67-69, 72-73,
    74-75, 77, 87, 90, 94, 116l 117-
    119
    immigration advertising, 61, 63,
    64-65
    map, 68
    Department of the Interior, 69
Chapman, James, 72
Cherokee Indians, 19, 20, 31
Chickasaw Indians, 20
Choctaw Indians, 19, 20
Colour, 7, 10, 12
Confederate Government, 12
Conservative Party, Canada, 88, 89
    see also Borden, Robert
Constitution, American, 14, 15, 35
    Fifteenth Amendment, 14, 15
Creek (Muskogee) Indians, 19, 20,
    26, 27, 32, 33
Cruce, Lee, 41, 43, 60

D

Daily Oklahoman, 36, 37, 40, 43
Dawes Act, 24, 31
Democratic Party, United States,
    14-15, 16, 24, 41
    Oklahoma, 36-37, 38, 41, 42, 43,
    44, 45, 49, 50, 51, 55, 56-57, 59,
    86
Disfranchisement, 15, 50, 53

E

Edmonton, 72, 112
    Board of Trade, 72, 76-77, 81-83
    United Farmers of Alberta, 83
Edmonton Bulletin, 71
Edmonton Journal, 75
Eldon District, Saskatchewan, 104,
    107-111
    see also Shiloh Baptist Church
    see Mayes, Mattie
"exodusters," 22

F

Five Civilized Tribes, 24, 26, 29, 31
"freedmen," 11, 12
free states, 9
Fugitive Slave Act, 1850, 9, 10

G

Garden, James, 46
Gore, Thomas P., 54, 56
"Grandfather Clause," 16, 53-54,
    57, 58, 59
Guthrie, Oklahoma, 38, 39, 92

H

Hamlin, Albert C., 50
Harris, Tom J., colonel, 82
Haskell, Charles H., governor of
　Oklahoma, 26, 39-41, 42-44, 46,
　47, 55, 59
Haskell, Murray, 26
Henryetta, Oklahoma, 46
Huff, Hazel, 78

G

Indian Territory, 1, 2, 18, 19, 20, 21,
　22, 23, 24, 26, 31
　migration to, 21

J

"Jim Crow", 14, 35, 36
Jones, John E., 87-88, 90
Jones, S. S., Dr., 93

K

Kansas, 9, 21, 22, 26, 38,
　slavery, 9
Kansas People's Party, 23
Klu Klux Klan, 13-14, 17, 21

L

Laurier, Wilfrid, prime minister, 88
Lawson, Richard, 61
Liberal Party, 88
　see also Laurier, Wilfrid
　Order-in-Council, 100
Lincoln, Abraham, president, 11
Lockhart, Mabel, 106-107
"Lodge Force Bill," 15
Lowrey, Seymour and James, 61
Loyalists (Tories), 10
　see Nova Scotia

M

Maidstone, Saskatchewan, 61, 63,
　102, 104
Marshall, R. C., mayor of Calgary,
　115

Mayes, Joe, 121-23
Mayes, Mattie, 121-23
McCabe, Edward P., 22, 23, 27
McCain, F. L., judge, 2
Miller, G. W., Dr., 95-9
Mississippi, 15, 16
　constitution, 16
　see also "Grandfather Clause"
Murray, "Alfalfa Bill," 26, 34-35, 38,
　40, 42, 43, 45
Muskogee, Oklahoma, 40, 46

N

Nova Scotia, 10
　schools, 10

O

Oklahoma, 1, 8 , 22, 26
　see also Daily Oklahoman
　see also Indian Territory
　land rushes, 24, 27
　territory, 24, 26
　map, 25
　see also Oklahoma Constitutional
　Convention
　politics, 27
　"Reds," 51, 57
　territory, 24, 26
Oklahoma Constitutional
　Convention, 34, 37, 38, 41
Oklahoma Enabling Act, 36, 40
Okmulgee, Oklahoma, 46
Oliver, Frank, 71-72, 76, 77, 79-80,
　87
　see also Edmonton Bulletin
Order-in-Council, Canada, 3, 100
Othello, 7

P

People's Party, Oklahoma, 51
Populists, see Kansas People's Party
Prejudice,
　British, 1
　Colour, 5-6, 7

see Devil
Canada, 10, 69, 75-76, 112

R

Racism, 1, 3, 12, 16-17, 18, 35, 124-26
Edmonton, 70-71
Republican Party, United States, 15, 12, 24,
Kansas, 22-23
Oklahoma, 27, 37, 38, 50-51, 53
Roosevelt, Theodore, president, 38, 40
Rosetown, Saskatchewan, 61
Saskatoon
Board of Trade, 83
Scott, W. D., 93, 94, 114-15
segregation, 7, 14, 35, 111
schools, 29-30, 35, 36,
see Sequoyah Constitution
see also " Jim Crow"
Seminole Indians, 20
Sequoyah Constitution, 26-27, 35, 40
Shiloh Baptist Church, 105, 119

S

Singleton, Benjamin, "Pap," 22
Slave owners, 9, 10
slave rebellion, 11
slave states, 9
slavery, 2, 8, 20
abolition of, 9
British, 2, 8, 9,

Canada, 9, 10
economics of, 8
see Kansas
North America, 8
South, United States, 8
Spanish, 7-8
United States, 2, 8
Sneed, Henry, 63, 73-75, 77-78, 88
Socialist Party, Oklahoma, 45
Speers, C.W., 93, 94-95
Stafford, Ray, E. 43
see also Daily Oklahoman

T

Texas, 14, 38
Twin Territories, 30, 31,
see also, Oklahoma and Kansas, 35

V

voting rights, 15, 16, 38

W

Walker, Bruce, 92-93
Ware, John, 70
Wildwood, Alberta, 63
Weleetka, Oklahoma, 73
Williams, Robert, L., 51-52, 56
witchcraft, 7

U

Underground Railroad, 9
Universal Negro Improvement
Association (UNIA), 116-17

Bruce Shepard has lived on the Canadian plains his entire life and has studied its rich past. His concern for equality of all peoples has led him to question, investigate and finally to tell this story of the blacks who sought their freedom in Canada at the turn of the century ... and the injustices they experienced. Bruce lives in Saskatoon with his family where he is the Director of the Diefenbaker Canada Centre at the University of Saskatchewan.